UNIQUE EATS AND EATERIES

OF

ATLANTA

Amanda Plumb

Library of Congress Control Number: 2020951753

ISBN: 9781681063140

Design by Jill Halpin

All images provided are courtesy of the establishments unless otherwise noted. Front cover images: Center—The Varsity, Ria's Bluebird, Heirloom Market BBQ, Little's Food Store, Refuge Coffee Company: Side—Talat Market, Miller Union, Dutch Monkey Doughnuts

Printed in the United States of America
21 22 23 24 25   5 4 3 2 1

DEDICATION

In loving memory of Aunt Patsy,
who taught me to love smoked mullet and leftovers for breakfast,
and frequently declared, "That's the best thing I've ever had in my life!"

CONTENTS

ACKNOWLEDGMENTS

In March 2019, I received an email from Naomi Stevens, an acquisitions associate at Reedy Press, asking if I'd be interested in writing this book. I was.

I can't thank Josh Stevens and the Reedy Press team enough for the invitation. Not only did they take a chance on me as a first-time author, but they also gave me complete freedom in selecting the restaurants and telling their stories.

I'm forever thankful to Jonah McDonald. The talented author of *Secret Atlanta* and *Hiking Atlanta's Hidden Forests* recommended me to Reedy Press and always makes himself available for advice on writing and marketing.

I'd like to thank my parents, Betty and Terry Plumb, for encouraging me to try new foods and appreciate the arts in all forms, including culinary. I was spoiled by my mom's cooking, a skill she learned from her Italian American mom, who was known for her lasagna, crabs and spaghetti, and other specialties. In addition to restaurant-caliber meals at home, we often dined out as a family, especially on Sundays after church.

When I was much younger, my parents and their friends had a supper club on Hilton Head Island. Every few months, the host couple would pick a nationality, research the cuisine, compile a notebook (this was pre-internet), and assign recipes to the other couples. Though kids were not invited to these dinners, my sister and I observed how you could learn about other cultures through food. That lesson inspired me to "travel" the world by exploring Atlanta-area restaurants, especially along Buford Highway or Jimmy Carter Boulevard.

I wouldn't have eaten at half of these establishments if it weren't for my friend, George Gussin. George and I share a passion for food and have shared countless meals together, most of them his treat. From fine-dining restaurants to food stalls tucked into the back of Plaza

Fiesta, we've eaten our way across Atlanta. One of these days, we'll finally start our food blog, *So Good*.

A big shout out to my dad, a retired newspaper editor, whom I enlisted as my first editor for this book. After writing each vignette, I sent it to him for review. In addition to catching typos, he'd occasionally add a word that I needed a dictionary to define or challenge my depiction of the Southern oyster industry. On every occasion, he deleted the Oxford comma, a habit ingrained in him after a lifetime living by the AP Style Book.

Most of the photos were provided by the restaurants. However, on a few occasions, I recruited friends to take photos. Thanks to George Gussin, Stephen Nowland, Adrienne Bruce, and Haley Zapal for stepping in as photographers.

And, of course, I want to thank all the restaurateurs, chefs, and grocers who shared their stories with me, as well as the marketing and PR folks who set up the interviews and located photos.

I wrote the bulk of this book in 2020, which means many of the entrepreneurs I interviewed were struggling to keep their restaurants open and adapting to the latest health and safety guidelines. It was a stressful and emotional time, especially for small businesses who had never before had to face such uncertainty.

This book tells their stories.

INTRODUCTION

When I was in the fourth grade, my family visited Rock Hill, South Carolina, where my dad had been offered a job. At the hotel, we asked the woman at the front desk to recommend a good Chinese restaurant.

"Rigby's," she replied.

"Rigby's is a Chinese restaurant?" we asked in disbelief.

"Ohhhhhh . . ." she answered in her Southern drawl, "I thought you said a good CHAIN restaurant."

That story instantly became a family classic. Why would anyone ask for a recommendation to a chain restaurant? Even at age 10, I knew local eateries were preferable to corporate-owned restaurants.

Don't get me wrong; a Pizza Hut Personal Pan Pizza is my comfort food, and anyone who has been on a road trip with me knows that I love Taco Bell. But those aren't unique eats.

Unique eats are dishes you can't get anywhere else, found in establishments that reflect the people who prepare them. They give you a sense of place.

Dining options were limited in my hometown, but Atlanta, where I have lived for more than a decade, introduced me to a rich culinary universe. Within walking distance of my house in East Atlanta Village are at least a dozen restaurants and bars serving tacos, pizza, burgers, ramen, poke, sushi, banh mi, and bi bim bop.

Atlanta is a city of transplants, and our food scene is all the better for it. Sure, we have our fair share of Southern restaurants, each claiming to serve the best fried chicken, but we also have street food from Thailand, Malaysia, Mexico, and Venezuela; peppercorn-crusted kangaroo from Down Under; and fresh bagels that rival any you'll find in New York City.

Nowhere demonstrates the diversity of Atlanta better than Buford Highway. To sample this six-mile stretch of global scrumptiousness, friends and I formed the Buford Highway Supper Club. We would visit a different restaurant each month. Seven years later, we had barely scratched the surface.

In 2016, I cofounded Chow Club Atlanta, an underground restaurant featuring a different cuisine every month. In working with immigrant cooks from across the globe, one constant I've found is that cooking is an act of love.

Over the past 18 months, I've interviewed more than 80 chefs, restaurateurs, and grocers to learn why they cook the way they do, who inspired them, and the obstacles they faced on their culinary journey. These stories are about love, family, failure, innovation, and reinvention.

In the midst of writing this book, the pandemic hit, and restaurants across the city closed their dining rooms. As weeks turned into months, the future of Atlanta's restaurant industry became less and less certain. But restaurateurs, by their very nature, are a resilient bunch. This may be the biggest challenge they've faced, but it's not their first setback. Atlanta is nicknamed "the Phoenix" because it rose from the ashes following Sherman's March to the Sea. I am confident that this book will be released in the midst of a resurgence in Atlanta's food scene.

My biggest challenge in writing this book was selecting only a few dozen restaurants to profile. There's so much good food in this city, and I'm sure every establishment has a story to tell.

You can learn so much about a place—and, more importantly, its people—through its food. Food allows you to tap into the culture of a place. I hope these stories will not only enrich your dining experiences, but also help you feel more connected to Atlanta, whether you're just visiting or have lived here all your life.

Atlanta is a unique city, steeped in history and offering unique eats aplenty. Enjoy.

UNIQUE EATS AND EATERIES

OF

ATLANTA

BELL STREET BURRITOS

The reluctant entrepreneur

When Morehouse College canceled his religion class in 2008, Matt Hinton did what any underemployed adjunct would do. He turned to burritos.

Matt's love of mission-style burritos is rooted in the late 1990s, when he was introduced to Tortillas on Ponce de Leon Avenue. "It was life-changing," remembers Matt, "totally different than any of the other Mexican restaurants I'd been to before." Tortillas epitomized the '90s underground/indie scene. The servers played in bands and sported tattoo sleeves. The walls were covered with concert flyers and band stickers. The burritos were cheap but tasty.

Matt was crushed when Tortillas closed in 2003, and he wasn't the only one. On their last day, the line was around the block. One customer ordered 52 burritos, so he could freeze them and have one a week for a year. As a consolation to loyal customers, the owners passed out copies of their recipes.

Fast forward to 2008: Faced with a significant loss of income and a family to support, Matt dusted off the recipes and asked friends if they'd pay him to replicate their beloved burritos. He figured that if he still missed Tortillas, others must, too. And he was right. In his first week, Matt had orders for 50 burritos, and West End Burritos was born.

The plan was simple. Customers would order via email, and Matt would deliver the following Monday. But on that first Monday, Matt burned the beans. With two hours left before the promised delivery hour, he started a new batch. It was 10 p.m. before Matt completed his last delivery. It was a pretty lousy day.

The last thing Matt wanted was to do it all over again the following week. But he did— each week for the entire semester. Even as West End Burritos gained popularity, Matt couldn't wait until the next semester when he could go back to teaching full-time.

Top left: While Bell Street is best known for their burritos, the quesadillas, tacos, and bowls abound as well. *Top right:* The Mission-style burritos are chock-full of fresh ingredients. *Above left:* For Professor Matt Hinton, making burritos was only supposed to be a temporary fix. Photo by Patrick Kolts. *Above right:* Green pork, chipotle steak, chipotle shrimp, and green chicken tacos.

The next semester, his class was canceled again. Meanwhile, journalists and food critics were asking about West End Burritos. He had a decision to make: quit or get legit. So he rented a booth at Sweet Auburn Curb Market and renamed the business Bell Street Burritos after the tiny street that leads to the employee parking lot at the market.

Four months after they opened, *USA Today* named Bell Street Burritos one of the top 10 burrito joints in the country. Today, the adjunct professor who started selling burritos out of his van is building a burrito empire, with three locations across the city so far.

Buckhead:
1816 Peachtree St.
404-815-0011

Tucker:
4053 Lawrenceville Hwy
770-417-8018

Inman Park:
112 Krog St. NE
678-732-9122

www.bellstreetburritos.com

Bell Street serves milkshakes made from hand-dipped ice cream, and, on Fridays, Lidia, one of the cooks, makes tamales from scratch.

BACCHANALIA

Matriarch of Atlanta's farm-to-table dining

San Francisco had a huge impact on Anne Stiles Quatrano, and through her, a huge influence on Atlanta's culinary scene.

Anne moved to San Francisco to attend the California Culinary Academy, where she met her future husband and business partner, Clifford Harrison. In the 1980s, she began cooking in kitchens across San Francisco. At the time, the most influential chefs in the city—Alice Waters, Judy Rodgers, and Joyce Goldstein—were women.

The couple moved to New York, where they often worked together, with Anne as the executive chef and Clifford as her sous chef. In 1992, when Anne was fired from one restaurant for "insubordination," the couple decided to move to Anne's family's farm in Cartersville, Georgia, where Clifford could keep horses.

The next year, they opened Bacchanalia in a small house in Buckhead. It was an intimate restaurant with dishes served on her grandmother's china. Although the couple had been cooking for years, they were new to the area and didn't have a reputation locally. Luckily, Gerry Klaskala of Aria and Canoe recognized their talent and tipped off the *Atlanta Journal-Constitution's* (AJC) food critic, Elliott Mackle. Soon Bacchanalia gained popularity as a "special occasion" restaurant, the type of place where you'd splurge to celebrate a birthday or anniversary. Their menu evolved accordingly, as they added items such as foie gras and sweetbreads to establish their new identity.

In 1998, Anne and Clifford decided to go back to their roots, opening up Floataway Café, a more casual restaurant featuring Bacchanalia's original menu. Anne describes the menu as "the food closest to our heart."

Today, their culinary empire includes W. H. Stiles Fish Camp and Star Provisions Market & Cafe, both of which provide high-quality

Left: Bacchanalia offers a seasonal menu that changes daily. *Top right:* Anne Quatrano and her husband Clifford Harrison are the chef/owners of Bacchanalia, Star Provisions, Floataway Café, and W. H. Stiles Fish Camp. *Above right:* Interior of Bacchanalia on Atlanta's Westside.

food at a fraction of the cost of Bacchanalia. Clifford spends much of his time managing Summerland Farms, which produces 20,000 pounds of produce and nuts for their restaurants.

With numerous accolades to her name, perhaps Anne's greatest legacy is the influence she's had on Georgia farms. Inspired by California's farm-to-table culture, from the start, Anne and Clifford sourced as many local, seasonal ingredients as possible. Although they were willing to pay top dollar for high-quality organic produce, there were too few growers in the region. The couple grew as much as they could on their farm and encouraged other farmers to do the same. By putting their money where their mouths are, they helped create a viable market for locally grown organic produce.

Bacchanalia &	Floataway Café	W. H. Stiles Fish Camp
Star Provisions	1123 Zonolite Rd.	Ponce City Market
1460 Ellsworth	404-892-1414	675 Ponce de Leon Ave.
Industrial Blvd., Suite A		678-235-3929
404-365-0410	www.starprovisions.com	

Unofficial headquarters of the Civil Rights Movement

As a soda jerk at Jacob's Drug Store, a hangout for Morehouse and Spelman students, Robert Paschal was convinced they would love his mother's fried chicken a lot more than the chow on campus.

His wife, Floreen, encouraged him to open a restaurant, but he didn't have that kind of money. Fortunately, she did. Unbeknownst to him, Floreen had been saving his earnings for years.

They opened the 15-seat Paschal's Sandwich Shop across the street from the drugstore, and word soon got out about Robert's fried chicken. On opening day, the line was out the door, which would have been great if the stove hadn't broken.

Robert called Floreen at home, and she started cooking. With no car, Floreen brought the food in a taxi, a routine they followed for almost two weeks until they had enough cash to buy another stove.

Robert's younger brother, James, gave up a position as a Pullman porter in Cleveland to become a partner in the restaurant.

Over the years, the Paschals expanded the restaurant. In 1959, they moved across the street to a bigger location. The following year, they opened a jazz nightclub like those James frequented while stationed in Europe. If men didn't have the required coat and tie, they could borrow one at the door. A racially diverse crowd, including the governor, flocked to La Carrousel Lounge to hear the likes of Lena Horne, Curtis Mayfield, Gladys Knight, and Stevie Wonder.

> If you've got a layover in Atlanta, you can visit Paschal's at the Main Terminal Atrium, Concourse A, and Concourse C of Hartsfield-Jackson Atlanta International Airport.

Left: Paschal's fried chicken was one of Martin Luther King Jr.'s favorite meals. *Right:* Paschal's contemporary dining room celebrates Atlanta's favorite son.

Back then, only two Atlanta hotels catered to African Americans, and both were across town. So, in 1967, they opened Paschal's Motor Hotel, featuring 120 rooms, a ballroom, meeting spaces, and a swimming pool.

One day, the Rev. Martin Luther King Jr., who had been eating Paschal's fried chicken since he was a boy, stopped by to ask for a meeting space for his civil rights coalition. The Paschals granted him indefinite use of a private suite. His favorite meal: fried chicken, mac 'n' cheese, collard greens, cornbread, and peach cobbler.

The restaurant was a popular spot for movement activists. When historically black college and university (HBCU) students were arrested during sit-ins, Paschal's staff would bail them out, feed them, give them a room, and have them call their parents.

Today, the nightclub and motel are long gone, and the restaurant has moved to a larger, more contemporary space in Castleberry Hill. The menu is a mix of old favorites and new chef-driven dishes, but the fried chicken and peach cobbler are as popular as ever.

180 Northside Dr. SW
404-525-2023
paschalsatlanta.com

SPRING

Less is more

It's surprising to find only 12 dishes listed on a menu, until you realize they're all incredible.

Kennesaw native Brian So grew up eating Korean food at home, but his love of the Food Network inspired him to experiment in the kitchen. He especially loved baking. He remembers the first dish he made while he was still in elementary school—pancakes.

In high school, Brian started working as a dishwasher at a Japanese restaurant. He worked his way up through every station. By the time he was ready for college, Brain was managing the kitchen. He realized that he was spending more time at work than in school.

To expand his cooking knowledge, Brian moved to New York and enrolled in the Culinary Institute of America. His world widened as he discovered previously unimagined levels of culinary mastery to aspire to. Next, he moved to San Francisco to stage (apprentice) at two Michelin-starred restaurants. When his father passed away, Brian moved back to Atlanta to be closer to his family.

After working in a few Atlanta restaurants (One Eared Stag and Sobban), Brian was ready to strike out on his own. For his first restaurant, he wanted something small and manageable.

He found the perfect spot just off the Marietta Square. Hidden away by the railroad tracks in the corner of an old freight depot was a small creperie. The tiny kitchen and 45-seat dining room were just what he was looking for. The architectural details of the historic building (exposed brick, hardwood floors, and sliding barn door) were simple yet elegant.

Brian intentionally has kept the menu limited, with four appetizers, four entrees, and four desserts.

Top left: Live Maine scallop crudo with green apple, watermelon radish, avocado, and lime. *Above left:* Pan-roasted Alaskan halibut with radish, turnip, pak choi, beurre blanc, and dill. *Center:* Chef/owner of Spring, Brian So. *Right:* Trains pass the old freight depot turned restaurant.

Though the menu is overhauled seasonally, it follows a simple formula. For the appetizers, there's always soup, a salad, a raw dish, and a foie gras. For entrees, there's one red meat, one poultry/pork, one fish, and one vegetarian option. He balances exotic proteins (lamb, duck, or quail) or with more familiar options (chicken or beef).

Brian's first love was baking, and it shows. He is as passionate about dessert as he is about the savory dishes. Typically the dessert offerings include one chocolate, one fruit-based, one pastry, and one sorbet.

Each dish is built around a single, seasonal ingredient. Whether it's dry-aged beef, Alaskan halibut, or a local peach, Brian lets the central ingredient shine by not overcomplicating the dish.

90 Marietta Station Walk Northeast, Marietta
678-540-2777
springmarietta.com

Don't skip the bread. Brian's sourdough is exceptional—crusty on the outside, spongy on the inside. It's served with house-churned, cultured butter.

MI BARRIO

Mi barrio es su barrio

Determined to create a better life for themselves, Jesus Lopez and his pregnant wife, Martha, hopped on their motorcycle and crossed the border from Mexico to the US. They made their way to Atlanta, where they heard houses were cheap, and settled into an apartment building affectionately nicknamed "Taco Town." Most of the residents in the complex were single men, so Martha sold plates of food to them out of their apartment.

In 1994, Martha and Jesus welcomed their youngest of five, Magdalena, and moved into a house on McDonald Street. Martha continued to cook for neighbors, but now there was space for customers to eat in their living and dining rooms. Most of the customers were Latino, except for a white cop named Paul. Concerned that the Lopezes would get in trouble for serving food out of their home, Paul urged them to open a restaurant.

In 2000, they purchased an old grocery store with a cafe, which would take them three years to renovate. On opening day, July 4, 2003, the Lopezes served 15 guests. Today, you'll be hard-pressed to find a seat during lunch among white-collar and blue-collar Atlantans, drawn by hearty portions and reasonable prices.

Mi Barrio is the quintessential family restaurant. Martha, Jesus, and daughters Lisa, Laura, and Magdalena do everything from cooking to cleaning. And don't be surprised if you see a kid or two running around or working on homework.

Restaurant life is exhausting, but the Lopezes try to find a healthy work/life balance. They close for a few hours between lunch and

> Vegetarian? Be sure to ask for the MacKrakin. Named for a regular, this taco sports rice, beans, chopped onions, cilantro, and avocado on a flour tortilla.

Top left: Corn tortillas are prepared to order daily. *Above left:* Jesus and Martha Lopez today. *Above center:* Jesus and Martha Lopez then. *Right:* On weekends, you can warm up with a bowl of Martha's Red Pozole, a traditional Mexican soup.

dinner to relax or run errands. Sometimes they close early, either because they've sold everything they prepared that day or because Martha needs a break. They're always closed on Sundays for church and family time, and once a year they take off a month so they can visit family in Mexico.

Everything is homemade, based on Martha's recipes from her homeland. The corn tortillas are prepared fresh for each order. Martha makes only 10 chile rellenos a day. "When they're gone, they're gone," explains Maggie.

Regulars know to ask about specials. Martha's red pozole is available only on Fridays and Saturdays. If she's in the mood, she may whip up pork chops or *bistec con pappas* (steak and potatoes).

On your birthday, the Lopezes will treat you to a shot of their very best Mexican tequila in an adult shot glass.

571 Memorial Dr. SE
404-223-9279

DUTCH MONKEY DOUGHNUTS

Gourmet doughnuts made fresh daily

When Martin Burge, who trained at the Culinary Institute of America, and his wife Arpana Satyu-Burge, who honed her pastry skills at the French Culinary Institute, moved to Cumming to be closer to Martin's family, they found jobs in different Buckhead restaurants.

After a while, the combination of a long commute and conflicting schedules left them too little time together. Not only that, they decided they wanted to work for themselves.

"You put so much heart and soul into it, and it takes up so much of your life," Martin said. "If I'm going to sacrifice so much, why do it for someone else?"

During his daily commute, Martin would pass a vacant space in a strip mall. He imagined the location would be ideal for a food operation he and Arpana could run together, but what would they sell?

Inspiration came in the 30 minutes the Burges drove to buy doughnuts at a favorite spot. Cumming needed a place that offered gourmet doughnuts.

In researching the subject, they learned that doughnuts originated in Holland. Combine that with their nickname for their youngest daughter, and voila! Their new venture had a name.

Ironically, Arpana, the pastry chef, focuses on the business side, while Martin experiments with possible recipes. Along with such standard favorites as chocolate sprinkles and raised glaze, the constantly changing menu may tempt you with such unique delicacies as Hazelnut Bailey's Buttercream, Black Forest Cake, Grasshopper Pie, Tiramisu Cake, and Cotton Candy Buttercream.

And you shouldn't overlook the namesake Dutch Monkey, which

Left: Kids love seeing how the doughnuts get made. *Top center:* Caramel Apple Fritters, Lemon Meringue, Lemon Bismarcks, and Dutch Monkeys. *Above center:* Husband and wife team Martin Burge and Arpana Satyu-Burge combined forces to create gourmet doughnuts. *Right:* When parents say, "Only one," kids love to pick out the biggest twists!

is filled with caramel custard and topped with chopped bananas and a dark-chocolate ganache drizzle.

"We make them the way your grandma would make doughnuts— if your grandma made doughnuts," Martin said. All the doughnuts are made from scratch, which is why they cost more than competitors'. The secret ingredient of the most popular item, the Apple Fritter, is fresh apples.

First-timers, accustomed to super-sweet, artificially flavored doughnuts, are often caught off guard. For example, the filling of the Lemon Bismarck is a homemade lemon curd, made with butter, eggs, and lemon juice. Once novices get over palate shock (it's bitter—like a lemon!), they usually can't wait for the second bite.

All doughnuts are made fresh daily. Martin arrives at 2 a.m. each morning to start baking. Your receipt advises you to eat your doughnuts that day, since they are made without preservatives.

3075 Ronald Reagan Blvd., Cumming
dutchmonkeydoughnuts.com

The menu changes daily, so check Instagram or Facebook to learn flavors of the day. Portholes to the kitchen allow you to see doughnuts being made. On weekdays, the best time to watch is between 6 a.m. and 9 a.m. On Saturdays, try between 8 a.m. and 11 a.m.

THE BUSY BEE CAFE

Southern soul food at its finest

As well known for its role in the civil rights movement as it is for its fried chicken, the Busy Bee Cafe has been a Vine City staple since 1947.

A self-taught cook from Carrollton, Georgia, Mrs. Lucy Jackson opened the small cafe at a time when it was uncommon for an African American woman to own her own business. The original cafe was located in a tiny space on Hunter Street (since renamed Martin Luther King Jr. Drive), adjacent to its current, much larger, location.

"Mamma Lucy" was known to take care of everyone. Once, when a visiting African missionary was refused service because she was broke, someone suggested Mamma Lucy would take care of her. Not only did Mrs. Lucy feed the missionary for free, but she also sat down at the table to keep her company. In return, the missionary blessed the Busy Bee Cafe, asking that it would always stay busy. So it has.

In 1968, Mama Lucy sold the Bee to two Auburn Avenue businessmen. Looking to save money, the new owners cut corners in the kitchen by introducing ingredients from canned goods, instead of cooking everything from fresh ingredients.

Milton Gates, who grew up in Vine City frequenting the Busy Bee Cafe, purchased the cafe in the early '80s. Under Milton's "kick the can out of the kitchen" policy, the Busy Bee returned to cooking everything from scratch. Diners soon noted a decided improvement in the quality and taste.

> Cornbread is baked fresh daily. Any leftovers are turned into cornbread dressing the next day. And the lemonade is fresh squeezed in-house.

Left: Southern comfort dishes abound at Busy Bee Cafe. *Top center:* Who can resist a creamy Baked Macaroni & Cheese? *Above center:* A slice of Red Velvet Cake is the perfect ending to any Southern meal. *Top right:* All vegetables are prepared from scratch at the Busy Bee Cafe. *Above right:* Busy Bee prides themselves on their Signature Fried Chicken.

Today, Milton's daughter Tracy honors her father's and Mamma Lucy's legacies by using only fresh ingredients. The cooks understand how produce changes with the seasons and tweak their recipes accordingly. For example, in months when sweet potatoes are naturally less sweet, they add sugar.

The Busy Bee's Signature Fried Chicken combines Tracy's recipe with her grandmother's brining technique. The chicken is brined for 12 hours before it's coated in seasoned flour and fried in peanut oil. By far their most popular dish on the menu, it consistently appears on lists of the best fried chicken in the city.

Located near the four HBCUs comprising Atlanta University Center, the Bee was a popular meeting spot for leaders in the civil rights movement. Until he passed, Hosea Williams himself stopped in every Thursday for ham hocks.

Today, Busy Bee is a popular tourist destination for visitors wanting a taste of traditional Southern cooking—and history.

810 Martin Luther King Jr. Dr. SW
404-525-9212
thebusybeecafe.com

Disco Italian

Professor Giovanni grew up in Venice, Italy, where his mother owned a restaurant. After traveling the world playing soccer for the Italian national team, he entered the Miami restaurant scene, serving the likes of Frank Sinatra, Joe DiMaggio, and Luciano Pavarotti.

He met his wife, Gale Parker, in Atlanta, where the two of them eventually owned a restaurant. They weren't planning on opening another, but they stumbled across a little Italian restaurant in Inman Park and decided to buy it.

Before they officially opened their doors, a man stopped by to ask for a donation for an auction at his daughter's preschool. They donated a dinner for four. The man was so touched, he brought his wife and daughter for dinner that evening, becoming il Localino's first customers.

Il Localino, which means the 'little place" in Italian, has two secret ingredients: great food and an uncanny ability to make the dining experience unique by changing things up.

Only newbies order from the menu. Regulars know to order the specials, because whatever Giovanni is in the mood to make, whether it's homemade ravioli to calf liver Venetian-style, is what you want.

Professor Giovanni created Pappardelle Sinatra (homemade pasta with a sauce of roasted tomato, olive oil, fresh basil, and diced pancetta) as a late night meal for Ol' Blue Eyes himself.

Food isn't the only thing Instagram-worthy. Customers start snapping photos as soon as they see the string lights, colorful paper lanterns, and framed photos of Giovanni with celebrity patrons that plaster the walls.

> It's not on the menu, but you can order a half size of any pasta as an appetizer.

Top left: Professor Giovanni pulls inspiration for his dishes from across Italy. *Above left:* Rigatoni Bolognese, house-made rigatoni covered in the classic meat-based sauce from the city of Bologna. *Top center:* Osso Bucco, a specialty of Lombard cuisine of cross-cut veal shanks braised in white wine and broth. *Right:* Every night is a party at il Localino.

Like the menu, the decor is always changing. "We found ourselves getting tired of the same music and decorations each year," says Gale. "We like to change it to suit our taste."

To celebrate the Chairman of the Board's birthday one year, they played Sinatra all week and servers sported fedoras, a nod to Sinatra's signature trilby. By night's end, customers were wearing the hats.

Recognizing a good idea, Gale purchased 100 hats of all styles and hung them around the restaurant. At some point during the evening, music picks up, disco lights and the fog machine come on, and the hats come off the wall and onto customers' heads.

Since COVID, the hats have been replaced with disposable birthday hats, but the party atmosphere continues.

As for their first customers, the preschool daughter attends college, and the family still celebrates special occasions at il Localino.

467 North Highland Ave. NE
404-222-0650
illocalino.com

Tastes like it would in China

If you're looking for General Tso's Chicken or Mongolian Beef, there are plenty of American Chinese restaurants in the Atlanta area. Masterpiece is not one of them.

Although his mother was an excellent home cook, Rui Liu had no interest in cooking while he was growing up in northern China. He went to college to study hospitality management but changed his major because the field was overcrowded.

As a culinary arts major, he discovered a knack for cooking and food carving. After graduation, he quickly built a reputation as a chef and a food carver (he's even written three books on the art of food carving).

In 2008, a friend recruited Chef Liu to work at Tasty China in Marietta, Georgia. As a certified master chef, he was granted an O-1 visa, which is awarded only to "individuals with extraordinary achievement."

Although he knew the dishes he wanted to put on the menu, he soon learned American diners expect sugary dishes such as Orange Chicken. He was told "This is America, not China," and there was a standard formula for American Chinese menus.

Over time, he convinced the owner to let him add more traditional Chinese dishes to the menu. Customers loved the new choices.

"American people are the same as Chinese people," says Chef Liu, discussing the appeal of his dishes. "The mouth is no different."

After working in several restaurants, Chef Liu experienced the same frustration felt by many talented chefs who chafe under a system that puts the bottom line ahead of taste. For instance, he refused to cook with MSG, which he sees as a crutch for chefs of lesser talent. He wanted to do things the right way.

In 2014, he opened Masterpiece, where today he creates 140 dishes that "taste like they would in China."

Top left: If you're up for a little heat, try the Steamed Fish Fillet with spicy chili. *Above left:* Don't miss the Zhong-Style Dumplings, a popular Sichuan dish. *Center:* Masterpiece's award-winning chef/owner Rui Liu. *Right:* Zhangcha Duck (tea-smoked duck) is a quintessential dish of Sichuan cuisine.

And you don't have to take his word for it. Masterpiece has been named "Best Chinese Restaurant in Atlanta" by both the *AJC* and *Atlanta Magazine*, and Chef Liu has received two James Beard nominations.

For first-timers, Liu suggests starting off with Fu Qi Fei Pian, a popular Sichuan dish of thinly sliced beef tendon and tripe, served cold. Flavored with dried red peppers and Sichuan peppercorns, the Kung Pao Chicken may have more kick than you're used to. If you can handle the heat, the Boiled Fish Fillet with Ash Power and Chili is one of the few dishes with a whopping six chilis indicating its spiciness.

3940 Buford Hwy., Duluth
770-622-1191

11625 Medlock Bridge Rd., John's Creek
770-864-9110

masterpiece-chinese.com

Dishes are served family style, so grab a few friends so you can sample more dishes. Sichuan food is spicy, but you can ask to adjust the spice levels. Everything on the Tofu/Vegetable page of the menu is also vegan.

PLAZA FIESTA

A party for your taste buds

For Atlanta's Latinx community, Plaza Fiesta is a little slice of home. For everyone else, it's a chance to travel to a new country without leaving the Perimeter. For everyone, it's a one-stop shop for some of the most authentic Latin American food in the city.

The mall opened in 1968 as the Buford-Clairmont Mall. As Buford Highway evolved, so did the mall. In 1983, it was rebranded as Outlet Square, Atlanta's "first off-price shopping center," and in 1997, it was transformed into Oriental Mall. Two years later, it was almost knocked down to make way for a big box store.

Instead, Plaza Fiesta, the first shopping mall in the states to cater to the Latinx community, opened in 2000.

For immigrants from Latin America, Plaza Fiesta is a safe space where they can find community, comfort, and support. Thousands of miles from their homeland, customers flock to Plaza Fiesta to be surrounded by the smells, colors, music, and flavors they grew up with.

The interior resembles a Mexican streetscape. Although such stores as Ross Dress for Less, Planet Fitness, and Mercado Fresco (a Korean-owned supermarket that caters to the Hispanic community) anchor the mall, it's the six "markets" that create the feeling you're in a Mexican *mercado* (market). More than 200 vendors rent booths, selling everything from elaborate quinceanera gowns and piñatas of every shape and color to car stereos and travel services.

To navigate the markets, note that each aisle is identified by a letter, indicated on the floor, but it's more fun to meander through the aisles and soak in sights and smells. The central gathering space—the food court—is where the culinary adventure begins.

On your first visit, you may want to skip the pizza and chicken nuggets at Yami's Pizza, Gorditas & Wings, opting instead for

Left: Arepa Grill serves *patacóns*, fried plantain sandwiches filled with shredded beef or chicken, cheese, condiments, ham, and Venezuelan sweet coleslaw. Don't forget to dip in one of the creamy sauces. *Right:* In addition to sweets, Belen Candy Store serves fresh mango topped with *tajin* (a spicy and salty condiment) and *chamoy* (a sweet and spicy dressing).

the al pastor tacos, served on handmade tortillas. Or head to Mariscos Malecon Express for the ceviche (raw fish cured in citrus juice). Taqueria La Norteña, which serves a mix of Mexican and Venezuelan cuisine, offers arepas and empanadas that are not to be missed. On Wednesdays, you can't beat the 50-cent tacos at Las Recetas y Antojitos de la Abuela.

Hidden away near the back of Marketplace Five is a "secret" food court, with its own array of eateries. Every morning at Barbacoa Mexicana, a crew of women make tortillas from scratch to go with the stews. (They also feature what may be Atlanta's best burritos.) The Bar Tropical menu ranges from tacos and quesadillas to *huilotas* (quail) and *alambre* (grilled beef topped with chopped bacon, bell peppers, onions, cheese, and salsa).

Venture beyond the food courts, and you'll be rewarded with more delicious treasures. Aisle N (across from the main food court) is lined with such dining options as the Venezuelan Arepa Grill (order the Patacón, a sandwich made with slices of twice-fried green plantains instead of bread), Carnitas (with fall-off-the-bone, slow-cooked pulled pork), and La Fonda (try the whole fried fish).

Find your way to Aisle Q1 for some of the best tortillas in the market and a dessert of fruit in cream at Tropical Corner. Follow your nose to Soy Garapiñados, where the sweet smell of freshly caramelized nuts invokes memories of Mexican plazas and soccer stadiums.

With huge chunks of fruit, the *paletas* (popsicles) at La Niña Michoacana Pop are as Instagramable as they are tasty. Try such flavors as mango with chamoy, spicy tamarind, or pecan, and make sure to wash your paleta down with a refreshing fruit drink such as the lime, chia, and cucumber agua fresca. Ice cream lovers have plenty of options—Picos Ice Cream, La Moreliana, and Tres Marias, to name three.

Churros Mi Tierra fries up fresh, cinnamon sugar–coated churros, served plain or with your choice of 10 fillings, including *cajeta* (a thick, sweet confection made from boiled milk, nicknamed "Mexican caramel"), chocolate, *manzana* (apple), *guayaba* (guava), and *piña* (pineapple).

In addition to piñatas and candy to fill piñatas, Belen Candy Store creates custom fruit bowls. If you love mango but you're not a big fan of papaya, don't be shy about stating your preferences. Before heading home, pick up some traditional Mexican breads or a slice of tres leches cake from Squisito Bakery & Cafe.

Plaza Fiesta offers more than two dozen dining options, so visit on an empty stomach.

4166 Buford Hwy. NE
404-982-9138
plazafiesta.net

Top left: Taqueria La Norteña is just one option in Plaza Fiesta for traditional Mexican street tacos. *Above left:* Squisito Bakery Café serves a selection of desserts including tres leches cake and mil hojas (puff pastry filled with dulce de leche and cream and topped with your choice of fresh fruit). *Top right:* Popular Latin American desserts such as flan and *Fresas con Crema* (strawberries and cream) can be found at Squisito Bakery Café. *Above right:* Plaza Fiesta's food courts offer a variety of foods from across Latin America.

THE VARSITY

What'll you have? Think fast!

Two legends surround the birth of Atlanta's most famous fast-food restaurant: that Frank Gordy flunked out of Georgia Tech, and that a professor said he was too dumb to run a hot dog stand. Neither is true.

Gordy's mom sent him to Georgia Tech against his wishes. He had little appetite for college and even less for the chow. After one semester, he dropped out.

He and his brother went to Florida to cash in on the real estate boom. On that trip, Frank discovered an appetizing business concept—small restaurants that served food fast.

Returning to Atlanta in 1926, he purchased the Yellow Jacket Inn, a small restaurant on Luckie Street, that sold mostly hot dogs and chili, primarily to Tech students.

With $1,860 in profits from the Yellow Jacket, Gordy leased space next to the Georgia Tech campus and reopened his restaurant under the name that would become an Atlanta legend. He chose "The Varsity" because he had plans to expand to Athens, Georgia, and feared Georgia Bulldog fans wouldn't patronize a restaurant named for a rival mascot.

Over time, Gordy accumulated two city blocks. He would sell some land for the I-75/I-85 Connector, making The Varsity among the most visible eateries in America. To compensate for lost parking, he erected a two-story parking deck.

Originally, The Varsity was primarily a drive-in restaurant where patrons were served by African American carhops who recited the menu from memory. Until 1963, their only compensation was tips. The carhops, in fact, purchased meals from the restaurant and, in turn, had to collect from customers.

Left: When you reach the front of the line, be ready to answer the familiar question "What'll ya have?" *Right:* Hot dogs, rings, and a Frosted Varsity Orange are a classic Varsity meal.

The most famous Varsity carhop of all was Flossie Mae. He was known for singing the menu and for the flamboyant hats he wore. When he retired at age 86, Flossie had car-hopped at The Varsity for 56 years!

Today, The Varsity is still family-owned, run by the third generation. And while curb service is still available, most customers dine indoors. When the Yellow Jackets play at home, as many as 30,000 customers may be served in a day.

When the cashier shouts, "What'll you have?" be ready with your order or you'll be sent to the back of the line. Better yet, cut the chatter and order in Varsity vernacular. Hint: For a classic Varsity Meal, order a Hot Dog (comes with chili and mustard), Ring One (Onion Rings), and an F. O. (Frosted Varsity Orange).

Atlanta Locations

61 North Ave.
404-881-1706

6045 Dawson Blvd., Norcross
770-840-8519

2790 Town Center Dr., Kennesaw
770-795-0802

Hartsfield Jackson Airport
Gates C & F

Varsity Lingo

Hot Dog	Hot dog with chili and mustard
Heavy Weight	Hot dog with extra chili
Naked Dog	Plain hot dog on a bun
MK Dog	Naked dog with mustard and ketchup
Regular C Dog	Hot dog with ketchup
Red Dog	Naked dog with ketchup
Yellow Dog	Naked dog with mustard
Yankee Dog	Plain dog with mustard
Walk a Dog	Hot dog to go
Steak	Hamburger with ketchup, mustard, and pickle
Chili Steak	Hamburger with chili
Glorified Steak	Hamburger with mayo, lettuce, and tomato
Mary Brown Steak	Hamburger with no bun
Naked Steak	A plain steak
Varsity Orange	The original formula
N. I. Orange	Varsity Orange with no ice
F. O.	Frosted Varsity Orange
Joe-ree	Coffee with cream
P. C.	Plain chocolate milk always served with ice
N. I. P. C.	Chocolate milk with no ice
All the Way	With onions—Can be a hot dog, chili, steak, etc.
Bag of Rags	Potato chips
Sideways	Onions on the side
Ring One	Order of onion rings
Strings	An order of french fries

Top: The Varsity has been an Atlanta institution since 1928. *Above left:* Known for his outrageous hats, Flossie Mae car-hopped at The Varsity for more than 50 years! *Above right:* Crispy fried apple and peach pies are made from scratch each day.

CRAWFISH SHACK

Cajun food with a hint of Vietnam

Hieu Pham's first Lowcountry boil changed his life.
When the Atlanta native was 12, he visited family friends in New Orleans, where many Vietnamese refugee families had relocated following the Vietnam War.

Hieu can still remember his excitement from the first time he saw a pot of Lowcountry boil dished out on a picnic table. Credited to the Gullah/Geechee region of coastal South Carolina and Georgia, Lowcountry Boil (also known as Frogmore Stew) is a one-pot meal of shrimp or crawfish, corn, potatoes, and sausage, cooked in a spicy broth, often outdoors in a huge pot.

Hieu loved the meal, and, from then on, whenever the family friends visited, they'd bring along bags of crawfish to make Hieu's favorite meal.

Hieu studied interior design in college, but when he graduated during the height of the 2008 recession, job prospects were poor. When his parents asked what other career paths he might take, the first thing that came to mind was cooking seafood.

Fortunately, his family owned a strip mall on Buford Highway, a mecca for emerging cuisines in the Southeast. Initially, the Crawfish Shack offered take-out service only. The menu was simple, primarily Lowcountry Boil and fried seafood. His mom was the cook. His dad and younger sister also helped.

The first year, Hieu worked 12- to 14-hour days year-round, sometimes collecting less than $100. Hieu says he lost 40 pounds and most of his hair. But, word spread of their delicious fare, and soon lines of customers often stretched out the door. In fact, so many customers said they would return more frequently if they could dine in, that the family expanded the Crawfish Shack by building a dining room in the adjacent storefront.

Left: Cajun Boiled Crawfish served with corn on the cob, red potatoes, and hushpuppies. *Center:* Crawfish Shack chef/owner Hieu Pham. *Right:* The Shack-Tastic Platters come with Cajun boiled or steamed snow crab, crawfish, mussels, shrimp, andouille sausage, corn, and red potatoes.

Menu offerings have expanded over the years. In addition to the ever-popular Lowcountry Boil, you'll find fried and steamed seafood, including crawfish, shrimp, catfish, red snapper, grouper, oysters, soft-shell crab, and *swai* (Vietnamese catfish that tastes like grouper). Hieu is particularly proud of his Cajun Lobster Roll, inspired by a trip to Boston. And don't forget to try the po'boys.

Don't go to the Crawfish Shack looking for fast food. Some restaurants use pre-battered, frozen seafood, but the seafood here is fresh, displayed on beds of ice. You can watch the cook select your main course, then dust and fry the seafood. A key ingredient is a blend of spices, a family secret recipe that combines Vietnamese and Cajun flavors.

Looking for a little more Asian flare with your seafood? Check out BonTon in Midtown. Hieu opened this lively Viet-Creole spot with partners Eric Simpkins (the Lawrence) and Darren Carr (Top Flr). With an extensive cocktail menu, BonTon could be at home on Bourbon Street. If you go, don't miss the Five-Spice BBQ Shrimp, the Nashville Hot Oyster Roll, or the Charbroiled Crab Claws.

Crawfish Shack
4337 Buford Hwy. NE
404-329-1610
crawfishshackseafood.com

BonTon
674 Myrtle Dr.
404-996-6177
bontonatl.com

Add a little kick to your fries by sprinkling on some Louisiana fish fry spices, available on each table.

SWEET AUBURN CURB MARKET

The People's market

A year after the Great Atlanta Fire of 1917 ravaged Old Fourth Ward, a group of women approached the city about creating a public marketplace. The following May, the Municipal Market opened as an empty lot where farmers sold produce from wagons and tents.

When the existing brick structure was built in 1924, African American farmers were not allowed to sell inside. Instead, they sold their produce on the curb outside of the building, hence the nickname "Sweet Auburn Curb Market" or, simply, the Curb Market.

Today, the City of Atlanta owns the building, the nonprofit Municipal Market Co. runs the market, and the stalls are independently owned.

The clientele reflects Atlanta's population. You'd be hard-pressed to find another spot where people shopping with EBT cards rub shoulders with customers wearing business suits and Grady Hospital staffers in scrubs. According to Pamela Joiner, Curb Market general manager, "No matter who you are or where you're from, there's something for everyone at The Curb Market."

The three meat counters sell every part of the pig, from snout to tail. In fact, if you want to go whole-hog, you can buy an entire pig. Three Korean-owned produce vendors cater to their Southern customers with enormous bags of collards, which can be chopped to order—perfect for Sunday supper or a holiday feast.

> The Atlanta Streetcar stops right in front of the market, or you can validate your parking ticket for one free hour of parking.

Left: Miss D started selling her pralines in 2009 with a 4 ft. table and now has two locations and eight kiosks inside the Mercedes Dome. *Center:* You can find the original exterior sign hanging inside the market. *Right:* Country Meat, one of three meat counters in the market, has been a market staple for more than 40 years.

While a small grocery store (or "urban bodega") is the largest tenant, the 13 restaurants are the principal draw. You and your coworkers can't agree on where to have lunch? At the Curb Market, there's no need for consensus. With soul food, BBQ, arepas, Vietnamese cuisine, burgers, Philly cheesesteaks, handheld pies, and more, if you can't find something to eat, you ain't hungry.

Such variety is not the result of coincidence. To limit competition for vendors and to guarantee a diverse selection of cuisines for customers, prospective tenants may not duplicate a cuisine already represented in the market.

The Municipal Market serves as an incubator for new food entrepreneurs. Rent is modest compared to the cost of a freestanding building. Plus, foot traffic is built in. Arepia Mia, Bell Street Burritos, Grindhouse Burgers, Sweet Auburn BBQ, and Just Add Honey all are enterprises that began here and now have locations across the city.

The food stall owners support each other. On one occasion when a tenant was left short-staffed because an employee quit unexpectedly, other restaurants rallied, lending their own workers until a replacement could be hired.

209 Edgewood Ave. SE
404-659-1665
municipalmarketatl.com

MILLER UNION

Seasons eatings

During the '90s, Steven Satterfield and Neal McCarthy worked, respectively, at Watershed and Inman Park's Sotto Sotto, where they sharpened their skills, Steven in Scott Peacock's kitchen and Neal managing the front of the house.

Each excelled in his area of expertise but lacked the confidence to start his own place. It was Neal's wife, Caroline, who saw the potential of the two men teaming up.

The concept they landed on was farm-to-table, a popular restaurant theme in recent years, but one that is harder to sustain in practice than it sounds. A true farm-to-table restaurant flows with the local harvest, which means the menu must change with the growing season. According to Steven, Georgia has six growing seasons: fall, winter, spring, early summer, middle summer, and late summer.

While the protein offerings may be consistent, the vegetables and fruit evolve with the seasons, which is why Steven makes in-season produce the star of every dish.

"We treasure the ingredients and express it in the best way possible, whether that's a different technique or just leaving it alone," says Steven.

The only dish that has been on the menu since day one is their Farm Baked Egg. A variation on the coddled egg, this dish consists of an egg baked in cream infused with celery, sweet onion, thyme, parsley, and peppercorn. The egg whites solidify with the cream while the yolk remains runny—perfect for soaking up with rustic bread.

"The sum is greater than its parts," Steven says.

While Steven focuses on the kitchen, Neal creates the dining experience for guests.

"I want people to feel at home, like this is your dining room, but at a restaurant where you're taken care of," Neal says.

Left: James Beard award–winning chef Steven Satterfield is the executive chef and co-owner of Miller Union. Photo by Heidi Geldhauser. *Center:* The seasonal vegetable plate showcases local, farm-fresh ingredients. Photo by Craig Brimanson. *Top right:* General manager and co-owner Neal McCarthy leads the dining room and the wine program. Photo by Heidi Geldhauser. *Above right:* The Farm Baked Egg in celery cream has been on the menu since day one. Photo by Craig Brimanson.

There was always a bottle of wine on his family's table when Neal was growing up, so he's worked hard to stock the Miller Union wine list with affordable options. He sniffs out vineyards that follow sustainable practices and don't overly manipulate the grapes, allowing the essence of the soil, sun, and water to emerge.

Miller Union's wine list is constantly changing, so if you have a favorite wine you don't see, tell your server.

And because no dining experience is complete without dessert, the pastry chef creates stunningly delicious plates using in-season ingredients (of course) to complement the rest of the menu.

999 Brady Ave. NW
678-733-8550
millerunion.com

Steven won the James Beard Foundation's "Best Chef: Southeast" award in 2017, and Miller Union has either been a finalist or semifinalist for the James Beard Foundation's "Outstanding Wine Program" for five years in a row.

SEVANANDA NATURAL FOODS MARKET

Atlanta's oldest (and only) retail food co-op

The name Sevananda is Sanskrit for "service is bliss." It was founded in 1974 by members of the Ananda Marga, a spiritual community that focuses on yoga, meditation, and serving others. Members follow a plant-based diet. They established Sevananda to pool purchasing power for natural products that weren't widely available in Atlanta at the time.

Initially, Sevananda's profits went to the community's international headquarters, but in 1995, they reorganized as a co-op in order to keep proceeds in the community.

Anyone can join the co-op. A lifetime membership is currently $120 and may be paid by installment. Membership includes free events, discounts on classes, a monthly 10 percent discount, special prices on select items, and voting rights at the annual membership meeting. Also, in years when the co-op is in the black, members may receive a refund at year's end.

Everyone is welcome to shop at Sevananda. You don't need to be a member/owner.

Sevananda strictly adheres to policies about products they carry. Almost all products sold are organic. They shun artificial

Each month, Sevananda supports a nonprofit through their Be the Change program. Customers are encouraged to round up their bill to the nearest dollar and donate the change to the organization. In addition, Sevananda promotes the organization's work in a display at the front of the store and invites the nonprofit to set up an info table at the store.

Left: Sevananda has the largest selection of dried herbs in the city. *Center:* Sevananda offers a wide assortment of vegan and vegetarian grab-and-go options. *Right:* The produce department features vegetables from local farms. Photos courtesy of Sevananda.

flavors and colors, toxic dyes, refined sugar (unless no substitute is available), and GMOs. Most noticeably, you won't find alcohol or meat on these shelves.

If you are looking for alternatives to milk, meat, or flour, Sevananda carries a wide selection. They also offer bulk groceries and nontoxic cleaning supplies.

The extensive bulk department offers candies, nuts, grains, flours, sugars, soup mixes, coffee, pasta, trail mixes, cereals, soaps, olive oil, soy sauce, almond and peanut butter (freshly ground to order!), and even local honey. You can buy as much or as little as you'd like and know that you are helping the environment by eliminating most packaging.

The hot bar offers vegan and vegetarian dishes for breakfast, lunch, and dinner. Start your morning off with vegan scramble, grits, and biscuits. Among the more popular grab-and-go items, you will find the Tofu Enlightenment Wrap, spicy collards, and vegan mac 'n' cheese. The vegan cinnamon rolls and banana bread are baked in-house.

The wellness department carries cruelty-free beauty products, health supplements, herbal remedies, vitamin supplements, aromatherapy oils, and tinctures. The herb wall offers more than 300 different culinary and medicinal herbs—the largest selection in Atlanta.

For those who want to learn more about living a healthy lifestyle, Sevananda offers classes on food safety, holiday vegan cooking, raw foods, fermentation, yoga, and meditation. Classes are open to the public and free for members/owners.

467 Moreland Ave. NE
404-681-2831
sevananda.coop

THE TAMARIND GROUP

The Niyomkul's Thai empire

Atlanta can thank Nan and Charlie Niyomkul for introducing us to Thai cuisine beyond pad thai and panang curry.

Nan learned to cook working alongside her mother, a street food vendor in Bangkok. Charlie began working in hotels at age 14. The two high school friends moved to New York City, where Charlie studied hospitality at Cornell and Nan worked three jobs to support him.

Eventually, the two married and opened their first restaurant, Tamarind, a family-style bistro in Manhattan. Nan cooked. Charlie ran the front of the house.

On trips to visit their son at the Savannah College of Art and Design in Atlanta, Charlie saw opportunity. The city was slated to host the Olympics, and major companies were moving their headquarters south.

In 1995, they moved to Atlanta to try to replicate the success they had achieved with Tamarind. Though popular with diners, the real estate market undid Tamarind. After moving to Colony Square and reopening as Tamarind Seed, the second version of their bistro closed in 2019.

Luckily for Atlanta diners, Tamarind will reopen in 2022 in its original location. In the meantime, the Niyomkuls opened three new concepts, starting with Nan Thai Fine Dining in 1997.

As the name suggests, Nan elevates Thai food to the level of fine dining by combining traditional Thai techniques and flavors with high-end ingredients and impeccable service. Nan replaces the pork traditionally found in Hung Lay Curry with slow-braised lamb shank. She serves Pla Sahm Rod with pan-roasted Chilean sea bass and three-flavored chili sauce, crispy okra, bean curd, green beans, and eggplant. The pan-seared jumbo prawns and sea scallops in the Panang Talay are ginormous.

Left: Plah Pla Meuk—grilled marinated octopus in lime juice tossed with roasted chili paste, lemongrass, kaffir lime, shallots, cilantro, and mint, over bibb lettuce at Chai Yo Modern Thai. *Left center:* Chef DeeDee Niyomkul owns Tuk Tuk Thai Food Loft and Chai Yo Modern Thai. *Right center:* Nan's Lamb Hung Lay—slow-braised lamb shank simmered in Northern Thai red curry, peanuts, potatoes, and ginger. *Right:* Chef Nan is the matriarch of the Niyomkul family and Tamarind Restaurant Group. All photos courtesy of Andrew Thomas Lee Photography.

Daughter DeeDee grew up working in the family's restaurants, learning to cook from her mother and her grandmother. Today, she's owner of two Tamarind Group restaurants.

At Tuk Tuk Thai Food Loft, DeeDee transforms Thai street food into gourmet dishes. Sure, you'll find Pad Thai on the menu, but why not try Ba-Mee Moo Dang (egg noodles with BBQ pork, crushed peanuts, scallions, cilantro, chili powder, and yu choy—a Chinese green)?

At upscale Chai Yo Modern Thai, DeeDee offers a playful and contemporary take on Thai cuisine. She kicks up the Tom Kha (coconut soup) a notch (or two) by substituting chicken for lobster. And her father, Charlie, can't get enough of her Plah Pla Meuk (grilled octopus with chili paste, lemongrass, kaffir lime, shallots, cilantro, and mint).

Nan Thai Fine Dining	Tuk Tuk Thai Food Loft	Chai Yo Modern Thai
1350 Spring St.	1745 Peachtree St. NE	3050 Peachtree Rd. NW
404-870-9933	(upstairs)	404-864-7980
nanthaifinedining.com	678-539-6181	www.chaiyoatl.com
	tuktukatl.com	

Charlie takes pride in training the staff on Thai cuisine, so if you're uncertain what to order, just ask your server, and they'll be happy to help you find the perfect dish. And, for an extra-special occasion, book Nan's Chef Table, where parties of six to eight are treated to a custom menu created by Chef Nan.

MARCEL & OCTOPUS BAR

Good eats, late

It's 11 p.m., and you're hungry. You don't want fast food, and bar food won't do. Where do you go at that time of night?

Marcel and Octopus Bar serve haute cuisine for the late-night crowd. Typically, Ford Fry's Marcel is a splurge restaurant. This upscale steakhouse (where steaks run between $48 for an 8-ounce New York strip and $173 for a 42-ounce porterhouse that serves three) is the type of place you may go to celebrate an anniversary or graduation. But if you manage to stay awake until after 11 p.m. on weekends, Marcel offers a more affordable but still high-quality menu into the wee hours.

Even late into the night, Marcel is quite the scene, so don't expect to get seated right away. While you won't find Marcel's Reserve Burger (dry-aged with gruyere and bone marrow) on the late-night menu, you will find a classic bacon cheeseburger, steak fries, and a hot fudge sundae.

Octopus Bar, the brainchild of Nhan Le and the late Angus Brown, describes itself as "Punk Rock Fine Dining." And what could be more punk rock than opening at 10:30 p.m.? Perhaps crashing on your friend's couch? Octopus Bar does that too.

You won't find a sign for Octopus Bar because it doesn't have its own location. When SoBa, the East Atlanta Vietnamese noodle house, closes for the night, the covered porch area morphs into its hip alter ego.

While dominated by seafood, Octopus Bar's eclectic menu changes frequently. You may find a Maine Lobster Roll, next to Spanish Octopus, sharing the bill with ramen or Flatbread with Sicilian Anchovy. For the adventurous eater, the Salt and Pepper Shrimp, served shell-on, is not to be missed.

Left: Marcel's Frites Canard are topped with chicken gravy and cheese curds. Photo by Mary Caroline Russell. *Right:* The Marcel Stack, a sandwich of pan-fried bologna and American cheese, shows up on Marcel's late-night weekend menu.

With last call at 2:15 a.m, Octopus Bar is a great place to finish a night of barhopping in East Atlanta Village or to refuel for round two.

Of course, you don't need to wait until late night. SoBa offers Vietnamese classics such as *pho* (noodle soup), *bun* (cold rice vermicelli salad), and *com* (dishes served with broken Jasmine rice). On weekends, their Hangover Helper of a bowl of pho and a Bloody Mary, may be just what you need to recover from your late-night adventures.

Marcel
1170 Howell Mill Rd.
404-665-4555
marcelatl.com

Octopus Bar
560 Gresham Ave. SE
octopusbaratl.com

SoBa
560 Gresham Ave. SE
404-627-9911
soba-eav.com

ANN'S SNACK BAR

Home of the Ghetto Burger

Anyone who visited Ann's Snack Bar when Ann Price was still alive will not be surprised to learn that she was pretty bossy as a kid.

"It was her way or the highway," remembers her younger brother James. Growing up in Sylvania, Georgia, the fourth of 11 kids, Ann was always a rebel who played by her own rules and insisted that others play by them too.

After high school, Ann put herself through Beauty Culture School by working in restaurants. She soon realized that she preferred restaurants to beauty parlors. In 1974, she purchased a Tasty Dog franchise, later renaming it Ann's Snack Bar.

Ann served hot dogs and hamburgers, putting her in direct competition with fast-food chains that benefited from national marketing campaigns and economies of scale. It was a customer who suggested she set herself apart from her competitors by spicing up the menu.

"You're in the hood," he said. "You should call it a 'hood burger' or 'ghetto burger.'" In 2007, the *Wall Street Journal* named the Ghetto Burger the best burger in the US.

There's nothing fancy about Ann's. Most of the seating is plastic chairs at folding tables on the screen porch. But the best (and only) seats in the house have always been the eight seats at the counter. Back in the day, these were front row seats for watching Miss Ann hold court while she shook her huge shaker of special seasoning

> The famous Ghetto Burger is one pound of beef (two patties), two slices of cheese, housemade chili, lettuce, tomato, onion, mustard, mayonnaise, ketchup, and bacon on a browned bun.

Left: Ann's Snack Shop is the home of the famous Ghetto Burger. *Right:* Ann Price was known for running the Snack Shop with an iron fist.

blend on the patties as they sizzled on the griddle. This was not fast food. Ann took her time and did things her way.

Perhaps more famous than her burgers was Ann's fiery personality. She had a list of rules and she was known to enforce them. Customers are not allowed to lay, lean, or put babies on the counter; consume alcohol or smoke; park illegally; allow children to slide on rails; stand at the counter when seats are available; curse; and, of course, no shoes, no shirt, no service.

Why all the rules? James remembers that when his sister opened the snack bar, Memorial Avenue was a rough neighborhood, and it didn't help that it was located right next to a liquor store. Ann created each rule in reaction to a specific situation.

When Ann passed in 2015, she left the snack bar to a few of her siblings. Although the menu hasn't changed, they have made some allowances such as accepting credit cards and allowing customers to call in orders. Ann's rules are still predominantly displayed, reminding everyone who's still in charge.

1615 Memorial Dr. SE
404-687-9207

HOLEMAN & FINCH PUBLIC HOUSE

The most sought-after burger in Atlanta

When Chef Linton Hopkins was opening up Holeman & Finch, he knew he wanted to recreate a British public house feel—a neighborhood spot where everyone would feel welcome. Well, that, and he wanted an excuse to experiment with all parts of the animal.

He created a "Parts" section of the menu, where, on any given night, you might find duck livers, fried chicken heads, and veal brains. He worried that if he added a burger to the menu, no one would order the more unusual dishes.

So from day one, although Holeman & Finch served a burger, it wasn't on the menu. Instead, they made just 24 burgers a night and only after 10 p.m.

Why 10 p.m.? Because he wanted to encourage industry folks to stop by after their shifts. "We're the professionals. Civilians want to eat at 7 p.m.," explains Hopkins, "We're the alternate universe; 9–10 p.m. is the time for great food."

And why only 24 burgers? Since everything is cooked from scratch each day, he would rather run out of an item than have to deal with leftovers the next day. All ingredients for the griddled double cheeseburger, except one, are prepared in-house daily: ground beef, buns, pickles—even the ketchup and the mustard. The exception is the one ingredient Hopkins says he can't improve upon: Kraft American cheese slices.

The gimmick took off. Soon, the bar was packed with people who were killing time until they could order a burger. And while it was good for the bar business, Hopkins came to realize it wasn't ideal for hospitality. Regulars were squeezed out by burger aficionados, who

Left: At one time, only 24 Holeman & Finch burgers were available each night starting at 10 p.m. *Center:* Chef Linton Hopkins of Holeman & Finch, H&F Burger, and Hop's Chicken. *Top right:* Chef Hopkins prepares roast chicken. *Above right:* Hand-cut beef tartare.

camped out for hours before the bewitching hour. Besides, the staff didn't like disappointing customers who wanted to order a burger before 10 p.m.

One day, Hopkins came across three generations of a family that arrived five hours early to wait for the burgers. In that moment, Hopkins decided he had enough of saying "no." He made burgers for the family, and from then on, whether or not they're listed on the menu, burgers have been available all day. Today, burgers also are available at H&F Burger in Ponce City Market, Trust Park, and Mercedes-Benz Stadium.

And while you can never go wrong ordering the most famous burger in the city, if you're adventurous, try exploring the Parts section of the menu.

Holeman & Finch
Colony Square
1197 Peachtree St. NE, Suite 160
404-948-1175

H&F Burger and Hop's Chicken
Ponce City Market
675 Ponce de Leon Ave. NE

holeman-finch.com

Burgers aren't your thing? Check out Hop's Chicken in Ponce City Market! Order chicken sandwiches or fried chicken by the piece (wing, drumstick, thigh, breast, or livers) or by the bird. You can even order a family dinner featuring a whole chicken, rolls, two sides, and two fried hand pies.

RIA'S BLUEBIRD

Breakfast from a champion

Aurianna "Ria" Pell was larger than life. You'd rarely find her without her signature Carhartt or denim overalls; newsboy hat; hair "high and tight, done right"; and tattoos peeking out from under her shirtsleeves.

The former bouncer was as tough as she looked, but she had a heart of gold. She did not allow substitutions (a rule many a staff member has tattooed on their body), and she'd let folks know if they were getting out of line. But she was also the first to help a friend pick up the broken pieces of their lives or to donate catering for a fundraiser. Ria championed a number of nonprofits, including the Atlanta Harm Reduction Center and Mondo Homo, an alternative queer art and music festival founded by her wife, Kiki Carr.

In 2000, long before the gentrification of Memorial Avenue, Ria and longtime friend Alex Skalicky converted an abandoned building that was once a drive-through liquor store (the drive-through window was replaced with a stained-glass window) into Ria's Bluebird, which today is one of the most popular breakfast eateries in Atlanta.

The made-from-scratch buttermilk pancakes are particularly fluffy, thanks to hand-sifting, and they're extra yummy when topped with caramelized bananas.

Ria's spin on the classic steak and eggs is her Brisket Breakfast: 14-hour, slow-roasted angus beef, shredded in its own spicy tomato broth, with two poached eggs and a toasted baguette.

> The line can get long on weekend mornings. If you can, arrive before 10 a.m. If not, write your name on the list, order a cup of coffee, and wait on the benches out front (not inside). Better yet, follow Ria's advice and order your brunch to go, and take it across the street for a picnic in historic Oakland Cemetery.

Left: Ria Pell was the larger-than-life personality behind Ria's Bluebird Cafe. *Top center:* Ria's buttermilk pancakes have been a fan favorite since the start, especially when topped with caramelized bananas. *Above center:* The Bionic Breakfast is a pile of skillet potatoes topped with sautéed mushrooms, grilled zucchini, red and poblano peppers, and a spicy tofu sauce. *Right:* Arrive before 10 a.m. to beat the crowds, especially on weekends.

Unlike many menus, where vegan and vegetarian options are an afterthought, at Ria's nonmeat eaters have plenty of options, including Country Fried Tempeh, Bionic Breakfast, Deep Dish Frittata, and (my favorite) Huevos.

In 2012, Ria made her hometown proud by winning an episode of Food Network's *Chopped*.

When Ria died suddenly in 2013 at age 45, friends honored her the way she would have wanted—with a huge party. The funeral procession was a mile long. As it passed the cafe, vintage hot rods did doughnuts in the parking lot. After they laid her to rest, everyone gathered at the Bluebird for Fox Brothers BBQ, live music, and a lot of booze.

Ria's business partner, Stephen Gannon, and his wife, Julie Pender, who's been working at Ria's for longer than he has, run the restaurant these days. They keep Ria's spirit alive not only through her recipes but also by continuing to support their staff and the community any way they can.

Be sure to walk around to see all the bluebird-inspired art as well as a portrait of Ria painted by her daughter, Amanda.

421 Memorial Dr. SE
404-521-3737
riasbluebird.com

CAFE SUNFLOWER

Serving up everything . . . except meat

In the early '90s, Lin and Edward Sun were living in Asheville, North Carolina, and running two run-of-the-mill Chinese restaurants when Lin started on her spiritual journey. She began following Ching Hai, a Vietnamese spiritual leader who founded Loving Hut, a chain of vegan restaurants with 200 locations in 35 countries (including two in the Atlanta area).

Inspired by her mentor's compassion for animals, Lin urged her family to become vegans. But she didn't stop there. Lin wanted to open a vegan restaurant. Thinking Asheville was too small a market for a vegetarian restaurant (this was, after all, the early '90s, before "plant-based" was a household word)—fortunately for us—they chose Atlanta for their venture.

The first few months were rough. Perhaps it was because vegetarianism was too niche at the time. Lin and Edward were so discouraged, they considered closing. After a few months, however, word began to spread and business picked up. In fact, Cafe Sunflower became so popular that they opened a second location in Buckhead in 1997.

The Buckhead location, currently their only location, has a contemporary vibe with abstract art painted by Lin. Her father built the booths, wine racks, and host stands.

Instead of focusing on a single cuisine, the Suns believed a multicultural menu would make vegetarian food more appealing to a broader base of customers. For this reason, dishes span the globe, taking inspiration from Italian, American, Thai, Chinese, and Mediterranean cuisines. The most popular dishes are the Soy "Chicken" and the "Bacon Burger."

A few years ago, the Suns revamped the menu to make it 100 percent vegan. Although it was relatively easy for the kitchen to find

Left: The Old Fashioned Chocolate Cake is so good, you'll forget it's vegan. Center: Cafe Sunflower owners Lin and Edward Sun. *Right:* Vegan Pad Thai is just one of the internationally inspired vegan dishes on the menu.

dairy alternatives, some customers were less quick to adapt. Some go so far as to bring their own cheese.

The desserts are not to be missed! Cafe Sunflower has had a longstanding partnership with Southern Sweets Bakery in Decatur. Lin worked with them to create the perfect vegan chocolate cake recipe. Annie, one of the Sun's three daughters, and general manager of Cafe Sunflower, remembers eating chocolate cake for weeks until Mom perfected the recipe.

Don't be surprised if you spot a celebrity or two. Benedict Cumberbatch, Lucy Lu, André 3000, Woody Harrelson, Missy Elliot, Amy Adams, Glenn Close, and Owen Wilson have all dined at Cafe Sunflower while in town.

2140 Peachtree Rd. NW
(404) 352-8859
cafesunflower.com

The Suns are happy to accommodate special diet requests. So whether you're soy-free, nut-free, gluten-free, or a Jain who doesn't eat root vegetables, Cafe Sunflower has a special menu for you.

NICK'S FOOD TO GO

No ketchup for you!

Ask any Atlanta chef where they like to eat, and they're likely to reply, "Nick's Food To Go." This tiny take-out joint offers some of the best Greek food in Atlanta.

Nick Poulos grew up in the neighborhood, where his father owned a liquor store. In the 1980s, Nick operated his own liquor store before he and his wife, Eleni, moved to Greece to raise their two daughters, grow olives, and produce olive oil.

In 1994, they moved back to Atlanta to open a burger place near "the projects." The menu was suited to the neighborhood: burgers, hot dogs, fried chicken, chicken livers, and wings. It didn't matter that Nick and Eleni had not grown up with the cuisine; their customers were quick to suggest a pinch of salt here or a sprinkle of pepper there.

As the neighborhood changed, so did the menu. Customers began asking for gyros, so in 2000, Nick added Greek dishes. They still serve burgers, but the Lamb Gyro is now their most popular item. Their Southern Gyro, a fried chicken wrap, marries the new menu and the old.

Each dish is made with care. Eleni makes a fresh batch of tzatziki every day and prepares the phyllo dough for the spanakopita from scratch.

While the gyros are by far the most popular item, the lasagna is a true gem. Made with noodles imported from Greece and a meat sauce that takes Eleni two days to make, the lasagna is one of the most labor-intensive items on the menu. Eleni makes a fresh batch every Thursday, but don't delay or you'll miss out.

Left: Evie, Nick, and Eleni Poulos—the family behind Nick's Food To Go. *Right:* Grilled Chicken Gyro made with Eleni's secret family recipes for marinated chicken and tzatziki.

Nick's Food To Go is a family business in every sense. In addition to Nick and Eleni, their daughter Evie, a cousin, and an uncle have all worked at the shop over the years.

Nick earned a reputation as the "gyro nazi" for his "this-isn't-Burger-King-you-can't-have-it-your-way" attitude. Rumor had it he would yell at you if you asked for ketchup on your falafel. Evie suspects Nick honed this tough-guy exterior while running the liquor store.

Don't bother stopping by Nick's after 7 p.m. or on Sundays; they'll be closed. "We value our family time, more than what we could make if we stayed open longer," explains Evie.

If not for the murals on the side, you might easily pass by this unassuming building. Most of the square footage is taken up by the kitchen, leaving just enough room for customers to place orders. You can eat at picnic tables outside or, better yet, bring a blanket and walk two blocks east to Oakland Cemetery, one of the most scenic picnic spots in the city.

240 Martin Luther King Jr. Dr. SE
404-521-2220
nicksfood.com

HEIRLOOM MARKET BBQ

A marriage of cultures

In the 1980s, Ji-Yeon Lee was the Britney Spears of South Korea—one of the original K-pop stars. She dropped her first album at 17, but by her fourth album, she was done with the stress and drama of the music industry.

She moved to Atlanta with her then-husband, where they opened and managed two restaurants. After their divorce, Ji-Yeon was determined to find something she'd be happy doing for the rest of her life. Although she enjoyed aspects of the restaurant industry, she was frustrated by being dependent on her chefs. So at age 37, she decided to enroll in the Cordon Bleu School. She loved it! "I felt reborn," she recalls.

During an internship at Repast, a fine-dining restaurant in Atlanta, Ji-Yeon met Cody Taylor, who had been working in restaurants since he was 15. The two found a connection over food. On their dates, she took him to Korean restaurants and explained such dishes as *bonchon* and *gogi-gui* (Korean BBQ). In turn, he took her to southern BBQ shacks and "meat & threes." They began cooking together, combining ingredients from their respective pantries. The couple found that the two cuisines blended well. For example, the savory and sweet Korean red chili paste, *gochujang*, has a flavor profile not unlike rib rub.

Ji-Yeon, still a household name in South Korea, and Cody were invited to film a cooking show in her home country. Along with a French chef, they traveled the countryside, sampling regional cuisines in home kitchens. That trip was a turning point for Cody, who felt burnt out after years of working in high-end restaurants. The experience reminded him of BBQ-tasting road trips he had once taken across the South. When they returned to Atlanta, he was inspired to open a small mom-and-pop BBQ restaurant.

Top left: Wife and husband team, Ji-Yeon and Cody Taylor. *Above left:* Don't be surprised if the line is out the door. *Right:* Each dish is a marriage of Korean flavors and Southern BBQ.

Tucked next to a liquor store, Heirloom looks like your run-of-the-mill BBQ shack, but the menu is anything but ordinary. How about a spicy Korean pork sandwich, topped with kimchi coleslaw and cucumber bonchon? In fact, Korean ingredients can be found in every dish: miso in the collards, Korean peppers in the mac 'n' cheese, and onion rings coated with tempura batter.

Ji-Yeon calls their cuisine "Atlanta-style BBQ" because, to her, it reflects the diversity of cultures in the city. Cody calls it "being ourselves," because "if you came to our house, this is how it would be."

2243 Akers Mill Rd.
770-850-1008 or 770-612-2502
heirloommarketbbq.com

The tiny parking lot gets packed at lunchtime, so stop by when they first open or after 2:30 p.m. And be prepared to stand. There's no seating inside, and it's SRO (standing room only) outside. Heirloom is BYOB, so pick up an adult beverage at the adjacent convenience store.

KROG STREET MARKET

Atlanta's first food hall

Sometime during the 2010s, food courts became passé, and food halls became the rage. What's the difference? Food courts, found in suburban malls across the states, typically are filled with chain, fast-food restaurants; food halls group local food vendors and mini restaurants under one roof in an urban setting.

Atlanta's first food hall, Krog Street Market, opened during the summer of 2014.

The 30,000-square-foot industrial space was constructed in 1889 as part of Atlanta Stove Works, which manufactured potbelly stoves and iron pans. The space sat empty for two decades before Tyler Perry opened his production facility, warehouse, and headquarters in the abandoned space. After 16 movies, 14 stage plays, and five television series, Perry moved out, and Krog Street Market was born.

As you enter, the high ceilings, brick walls, and concrete floor immediately signal the Market's industrial origins. Food stalls form the heart of the market.

The range of cuisines is remarkable. From sushi rolls and rice bowls at Makimono, fried chicken and hot chicken sandwiches at Richard's Southern Fried, to Asian steamed *baos* from Suzy Siu's Baos, there's something for every appetite. If French-inspired pastries from Little Tart Bakeshop are not your thing, then perhaps Indian street food at Jai Ho, Vietnamese soups and banh mi at Pho Nam, or Neapolitan pizzas from Varuni Napoli will tickle your palate. City folks are thrilled they no longer have to drive to Buford Highway for their beloved Gu's Dumplings (see page 166).

Parking at the market is limited. Avoid the lot (and work up an appetite) by walking or riding your bike on the Beltline.

Left: Customers dining at the counter of Fred's Meat and Bread. *Center:* The Meatball Parm sandwich from Fred's Meat and Bread. *Right:* The 1889 Atlanta Stove Works was converted into a food hall in 2014.

James Beard–nominated chef Todd Ginsberg has two stalls at the market. Yalla offers such Mediterranean and Middle Eastern favorites as shawarma and falafel, and Fred's Meat & Bread makes some of the best sandwiches in the city. Whether you opt for the Burger Stack, the Korean Cheesesteak, or the Crispy Smoked Catfish Po'boy, don't skip the garlic fries. And while you're at it, you might as well order the BBQ fries with white BBQ sauce or Old Bay fries with tartar sauce.

Finish your meal with an artisan chocolate bar from Xocolatl (see page 168) or a scoop (or two) from Ohio-based Jeni's Ice Cream.

And although the central food hall is always bustling, don't overlook eateries found along the exterior of the building. Watchman's (see page 78) has one of the best oyster happy hours in the city, Ticonderoga's (see page 152) Chuck Wagon Dinner is a rite of passage, and it's always tapas time at Bar Mercado. Ford Fry's Superica serves up a Tex-Mex menu, and Recess features mostly plant-based dishes.

99 Krog St. NE
Krogstreetmarket.com

In the business of welcome

One night over dinner, Bill Murray asked his wife, Kitti, "if the Bible highlights widows, aliens, and orphans as a group of people God cares about the most, why then don't we have friends that fit that description?"

At first, Kitti got a little defensive. Sure they were white, privileged Americans, but they donated to nonprofits and went on mission trips. They began to wonder what it meant to "love thy neighbor" when everyone around them looked like them. That night, they made a decision to move to a neighborhood where not everyone was like them.

They relocated to Clarkston, Geogia, "the most diverse square mile in America." This tiny town (1.4 square miles) is home to thousands of refugees, representing 40 nationalities and 60 languages. Kitti and Bill quickly made friends, both with refugees and native-born Americans. They learned there was a lack of good jobs in Clarkston, forcing many refugees to commute an hour and a half for low-paying jobs. As a writer who worked from home, Kitti lamented the lack of a coffee shop. She envisioned a coffee shop that would hire and train refugees while serving as a central gathering space for the community.

Kitti shared her idea with anyone who would listen, hoping someone would run with it. Finally, Bill convinced her she was the one who needed to fulfill her dream. In 2014, she assembled a board of directors and registered Refuge Coffee as a nonprofit. They crowd-sourced $3,000 to buy a used food truck from Craigslist.

Dave, owner of Clarkston Quality Motors, agreed to let them park the coffee truck on the corner of his lot two days a week for $1 a month. On days they weren't open, they took the truck to catering gigs. After Dave retired, Refuge bought the building. Guests still

Top left: Refuge Coffee is a welcoming space for refugees both as customers and employees. *Above left:* Thanks to Refuge Coffee, this old garage is now a popular community gathering space. *Right:* Kitti Murray has made her dream of a coffee shop that would hire and train refugees a reality.

order drinks at the food truck outside, but there's now plenty of seating in the former auto shop.

Employees receive a living wage while participating in a year-long training program, with classroom time and on-the-job learning. Refugees from Congo, Syria, the Central Africa Republic, Afghanistan, Burma, Morocco, Ethiopia, and Eritrea have graduated from this program.

Ask Kitti, and she'll tell you she's not in the coffee business; she's in the business of welcome. "Refugees have been violently unwelcome in their home countries. Through welcoming, we give back some of the dignity that unwelcome took away."

4170 E. Ponce de Leon Ave., Clarkston   145 Auburn Ave. NE

929-314-4837
refugecoffeeco.com

At the Clarkston location, no food is prepared on the premises, which means two things: you can bring takeout from nearby restaurants and you may bring your dog inside.

The backroom for Atlanta politics

In May of 2020, Manuel's Tavern was added to the National Park Service's National Register of Historic Places for its role as a social and political hub in Atlanta. The tradition goes back to Manuel's father, Gibran Maloof, who emigrated from Lebanon in the 1920s.

New to Atlanta and unaware of Prohibition, Gibran bought a bar across from the State Capitol. He came up with a work-around by selling beer-making kits. Following Prohibition, the Tip Top Billiard Parlor became a hangout for politicians and lobbyists during legislative sessions.

As a dark-skinned, Catholic immigrant, Gibran was never fully accepted by Atlanta's white community, but he was embraced by Black Atlantans. When white lawmakers wanted to connect with African American leaders, Gibran frequently served as liaison, brokering a newly paved road or sidewalks for the community in exchange for a meeting.

Several generations later, the bar from the Tip Top is the focal point for Manuel's Tavern, which Brothers Manuel and Robert Maloof opened in 1956. Manuel, who was stationed in England during WWII, found his inspiration in British pubs, community spaces where people congregate to collaborate and debate ideas.

On any night, you might find meeting here the Atlanta Fly Fishing Club, the Electric Vehicle Club of Atlanta, or Theology on Tap. The Atlanta Press Club met at Manuel's until the 1980s.

> Two parking spaces are reserved for clergy because regulars, the Archbishop of Atlanta and the Monsignor, complained about having to park so far away. Both have since passed through the Pearly Gates, but the privileged parking spaces remain for any member of the clergy to use.

Left: Manuel Maloof, co-owner of Manuel's Tavern, was active in the local Democratic Party. *Center:* Manuel's is a regular stop for Democratic politicians passing through town. *Right:* The bar is from Manuel and Robert's father's bar, the Tip Top.

The Georgia Production Partnership Group started as six people meeting at Manuel's, and legend has it that Georgia's film industry tax credits were negotiated here. As the unofficial headquarters for area Democrats, Manuel's has hosted countless campaign kickoffs, debates, and return parties.

Manuel thought an uncontested election was criminal, so when someone ran unopposed for DeKalb County commissioner, he jumped in the race—and lost. But later, he ran again and won. Manuel served for four years on the DeKalb County Commission, followed by eight as county CEO. He's remembered for pushing through Spaghetti Junction and for promoting people of color and women to top positions. Despite all that, he's best known for the iconic tavern that bears his name.

Manuel's menu includes an array of choices from burgers and fries to homemade three-cheese lasagna, with daily specials that range from fried chicken to a ribeye the regulars lust after.

There's no waiting to be seated. Pick your table. A server will find you. While waiting for your order, check out the photos and memorabilia on the walls and pay your respects to the regulars who never leave; their ashes reside behind the bar.

602 North Highland Ave.
404-525-3447
manuelstavern.com

Omakase-driven dining

Like many of Buford Highway's best finds, Sushi Hayakawa is tucked into a strip mall. But unlike many Buford Highway favorites, the chef is a James Beard Foundation semifinalist for Best Chef in the Southeast.

As a child, Atsushi Hayakawa dreamed of becoming a sushi master. He began training in the art of sushi at age 15 in the city of Sapporo on his native island of Hokkaido, Japan. Training to be a sushi chef requires time and dedication. Chef Hayakwa studied under a master *itamae* (chef) for years before he was allowed to prepare the sushi rice. To this day, Chef Hayakawa prides himself on his sushi rice—slightly vinegary and served warm.

Chef Hayakawa moved to the United States and worked in a variety of sushi restaurants up and down the East Coast before settling in Atlanta in the mid-'90s. He built a reputation for himself by working at a number of Japanese restaurants in the city.

In 2008, he opened Sushi House Hayakawa, which quickly became a popular sushi spot. So fans were surprised when he closed the restaurant in 2016.

But Chef Hayakawa envisioned bringing a more traditional Japanese *sushiya* experience to Atlanta. He renovated the space and opened Sushi Hayakawa. With just six seats at the sushi bar and five tables of four, Chef Hayakwa could offer a more intimate, *omakase-*forward dining experience.

Roughly translating to "respectfully letting another choose for you," *omakase* is the Japanese version of a tasting menu. Every night, you'll find Chef Hayakawa behind that sushi bar, his signature red headband around his brow. Giving complete creative control to Chef Hayakawa is a culinary adventure. You won't know what you'll be eating, but you know it will be of the finest quality.

Left: Chef Atsushi Hayakawa is the most celebrated sushi chef in Atlanta. *Top right:* Madai Aubri—torched red snapper. *Above right:* Uni Ikura Don, sea urchin and salmon roe over rice.

His relationships with fishmongers in the US and Japan enable him to procure quality products and special items not found elsewhere in the city. His Japanese Uni (sea urchin) is always high quality; the house-seasoned Ikura (red caviar) has been recognized as some of the best anywhere; and he's an expert with Ankimo (monkfish liver), the foie gras of the sea.

Among many of its accolades, Sushi Hayakawa was named one of the 12 most authentic sushi restaurants in America by *Men's Journal* and the fifth-best restaurant in Atlanta by *Atlanta Magazine* in 2018.

5979 Buford Hwy. NE
770-986-0010
sushihayakawa.com

Order the premium wasabi, grown here in Georgia, but be warned, you'll never be satisfied with the horseradish knockoff again.

SHAKESPEARE'S TAVERN PLAYHOUSE

Taming of the stew

On May 16, 1984, *As You Like It* opened for a one-week run at Manuel's Tavern. The production was staged by the Atlanta Shakespeare Society, originally a book club, which wanted to bring their favorite author to life in a more accessible setting than a traditional theater. Jeff Watkins, the director, believed a neighborhood pub was just such a place. Early productions drew widespread attention, including coverage by the *Wall Street Journal*, the *New York Times*, CBS, and CNN.

As the company outgrew Manuel's Tavern, Atlanta Shakespeare Society members envisioned a permanent space of their own, where plays could be staged in an informal setting and where food and drink could contribute to the experience. In short, they wanted to create a setting where the plays could be brought to life in a manner Shakespeare himself would approve.

Tucked between modern buildings on Peachtree Street, the Globe-inspired exterior of Shakespeare's Tavern Playhouse is the first hint that guests are in for a special experience. Inside, guests sit at tables where eating, drinking, and making merry are not only tolerated but encouraged.

Prior to every performance, patrons troop to the cafeteria-style kitchen to order such house favorites as Rainy Day Tomato Basil

> Because most performances sell out, order tickets beforehand. Seating is first-come, first-served, so arrive early! Doors open 75 minutes before each performance.

Left: From the street, Shakespeare Tavern resembles the Globe Theatre in London. *Top right:* Gusts enjoying a performance of *A Midsummer Night's Dream* at the Shakespeare Tavern Playhouse. Photo by Jeff Watkins. *Above right:* Ginger Carrot Soup with a side of Zucchini Bread, complete with Caramelized Onion and Gruyere Tartlet on the side. Photo by Michael Rocchins.

Soup and Beef and Two-Bean Chili. If British pub food is more to your liking, you may choose from such dishes as Shepherd's Pie, Cornish Pasty, or the King's Supper Sandwich (roasted pork loin, apricots, prunes, and rosemary butter on a baguette). Beer and wine may be purchased with your meal, and there's a full bar in the lobby. Desserts and drinks are available during intermission.

To date, the company has performed the entire Shakespeare canon twice. In addition, they offer other classic plays and never fail to perform Dickens' *A Christmas Carol* during December. They are passionate about showing audiences that Shakespeare doesn't need to be stuffy. Far from it. In the Bard's day, his plays were performed before often-rowdy audiences, common people who understood the double entendres and bawdy winks in the comedic plays and jeered the vile antics of villains in the tragedies.

Don't be surprised if, when you're just about to lift a brew, you find yourself being addressed by a cast member. You may not grasp the meaning of every word, but you'll be caught up in the timeless emotions that these plays evoke.

499 Peachtree St NE
shakespearetavern.com
404-874-5299

SUBLIME DOUGHNUTS

R&D never tasted so good

Growing up in Marietta, Georgia, Kamal Grant always loved sweets and pastries. When a Dunkin' Donuts executive presented to his high school food service class on research and development, Kamal was sold.

He didn't have the money to attend the Culinary Institute of America (CIA) like he wanted to, so he enlisted in the Navy as a cook. Four years cooking on the USS John Young, a destroyer, taught Kamal how to please the masses while making do with what was available. In the middle of the ocean for months at a time, it wasn't feasible to ship in fresh bread, so Kamal started baking for the crew.

Using the GI Bill, Kamal attended the CIA, where he learned taste, texture, and technique. At the American Institute of Baking, Kamal studied the science of baking, which helped him land a job at an industrial bakery in Atlanta.

One day, driving down 10th Street, he stopped by a new doughnut shop for a taste. It was terrible. A few months later, he saw a "for lease" sign out front. With his years of baking experience and culinary education, Kamal was confident that he could bake a better doughnut.

In the summer of 2008, Kamal cashed in his 401(k) and took over the store, equipment and all. With no budget for marketing, Kamal knew he had one shot with customers to make a big impression. So for the first year, he avoided the standard glazed and chocolate doughnuts. Instead, he opted for more memorable flavors — Reese's Peanut Butter Cup, Fresh Strawberry n' Cream, Orange Dream Star, and Sweet Potato Cake.

As a shout out to the ATL, Kamal created the A-town Cream, a Boston cream doughnut in the shape of the letter "A." When a navy buddy stopped by the shop to pick up doughnuts for his brother's

Left: Chef/owner Kamal Grant is always experimenting with new flavors. *Top center:* The Orange Dream Star doughnut, a play on an Orange Creamsicle, has a tangy vanilla cream cheese inside and a natural orange glaze on top. *Above center:* Spell out a special message in sugary sweetness. *Right:* Sublime has unique flavors you won't find anywhere else.

birthday, Kamal had an idea: if he could make the letter "A," then surely he could make any letter—and thus his "Happy Birthday" doughnut box was born.

Kamal continues his research and development, experimenting with new flavor combinations and techniques. His "burgers" are ice cream sandwiches with doughnut "buns." For April Fool's Day, he creates flavors such Mac & Cheese or Cricket that may sound like a joke but are really quite delicious. The Salt and Vinegar Doughnut (salted caramel with a balsamic reduction) was so popular that it's permanently joined the menu.

Georgia Tech:
535 10th St. NW
404-897-1801

North Druid Hills:
2566 Briarcliff Rd. NE
404-315-6899

sublimedoughnuts.com

Both locations are open 24 hours a day, but the fresh-to-order funnel cakes are only available from 10 a.m.–10 p.m. And be sure to ask about the super-secret mystery doughnut of the day.

MARY MAC'S TEA ROOM

Atlanta's dining room

After Mary MacKenzie lost her husband during World War II, she decided to support her young family the best way she knew how—by cooking. But in those days, it was almost unheard of for a woman to operate a restaurant, so Mary opened a tea room in a vacant storefront on Ponce de Leon Avenue. The year was 1945.

At lunchtime, the line stretched around the block. To make sure customers got their food in time to eat and get back to work, Mary handed out order forms to customers in line so their food would be ready by the time they made it inside. To this day, guests fill out their own order forms.

The second owner, Margaret Lupo, continued that tradition and expanded seating space by purchasing adjacent storefronts as they became available.

Subsequent owners have perpetuated Mary Mac's recipes and traditions. Everything is made in-house, from freshly husked sweet corn to hand-shucked peas. Fried Chicken is king, and no meal is complete without a helping of Georgia Peach Cobbler or Banana Pudding. If you're the indecisive type, steer clear of the Vegetable Plate. With more than 30 sides (including Fried Green Tomatoes and Mac & Cheese), picking just four might be too big a challenge.

Regulars often ask for their favorite server, some of whom have been at Mary Mac's for more than 40 years. Jo Carter, known for her signature back rubs, served as the restaurant's official Goodwill Ambassador until she retired in 2017.

> First-time visitors are in for a treat—a complimentary cup of Potlikker, the broth from turnip greens, and cracklin' cornbread for dunking.

Top left: The original Mary Mac's was in the corner storefront, but over the years, it's expanded, taking over several empty storefronts. *Above left:* Customers fill out their own order forms, a tradition Mary MacKenzie began. *Center:* Fried Chicken is the most popular item on the menu. *Right:* Mary MacKenzie opened the tea room in 1945.

Even with nearly 500 seats, you may have to wait in line. Among the 1,500–2,000 people who patronize Mary Mac's on a given day, you'll find regulars who order the same meal every week, families who have been dining at Mary Mac's for generations, and perhaps a busload or two of tourists.

Mary Mac's is also a popular stop for politicians and celebrities. But one of their most famous customers never set foot inside. Willie B., a western lowland gorilla and the darling of Zoo Atlanta for 39 years, loved it when her diet was supplemented with a gorilla-size portion of Mary Mac's cornbread.

Mary Mac's is the last of the 16 tea rooms that once dotted Atlanta. In 2011, the Georgia House of Representatives passed a resolution naming Mary Mac's Tea Room "Atlanta's Dining Room."

224 Ponce De Leon Ave. NE
404-876-1800
Marymacs.com

Atlanta's first taqueria

Like most boys in Guadalajara, Mexico, Martin Macias wanted to be a soccer player when he grew up. Thankfully for us, his eldest brother had other plans for him.

Jose, oldest of the 11 Macias children, worked in a factory in Chicago. When he transferred to Atlanta in the early '70s, Jose noticed a lack of Mexican eateries. So he quit the factory and opened his first restaurant, Acapulco.

The following year, Jose purchased El Toro on Buford Highway, a Tex-Mex restaurant that attracted American customers. Martin, his father, and three brothers moved to the United States to help Jose run the restaurant.

The youngest at age 11, Martin bused tables and worked his way up through every position except dishwasher. (He hates washing dishes.)

Over the next two decades, in what was nicknamed "Atlanta's Mexican Restaurant War," the El Toro chain went head to head with Monterrey, a chain owned by Raúl León, Jose's former business partner. To this day, a surprising number of Mexican restaurants in the region are owned by former employees of one of the chains.

When Jose decided to retire to Mexico, he left his restaurants for his brothers to run. Over the years, most Macias siblings owned at least one restaurant. Today, Martin is one of the few who is still in the business.

In the early '90s, Martin opened one of the first true taquerias in Atlanta, Los Rayos. Though ubiquitous now, at the time, it was hard to find Mexican street tacos, made with grilled meat and topped with cilantro and diced white onion.

After giving Los Rayos to his first wife in their divorce, Martin opened El Rey del Taco in 2002.

Left: Handmade corn tortillas are made in house by the hardworking tortilleras. *Center:* Martin Macias has been in the restaurant business for more than 40 years and continues to enjoy sharing his Mexican culture with his authentic menu. *Right:* The El Rey Del Taco Parrillada is the sharing platter, loaded with ribs, shrimp, chicken, chorizo, and melted cheese.

The two styles of tacos (mini and larger tacos on handmade tortillas) are the most popular dishes. Guests choose from over a dozen proteins, including *tripa* (chitlins/bowels), *cabeza* (cow's cheek), and *busche* (pork stomach). Each is served with cilantro, onions, a slice of lime, and two salsas.

Originally, the salsas were the standard tomato salsa (red) and tomatillo salsa (green), but a chef from coastal Guerrero, Mexico, introduced two creamy, pepper-based salsas to go with the seafood dishes. They were so popular that they've become the house salsas.

Meant for sharing, the El Rey Del Taco Parrillada is a platter of shrimp wrapped with cheese and bacon, short ribs, and grilled chicken and served with chorizo-topped queso and fresh tortillas inspired by Argentinian BBQ.

5288 Buford Hwy., Doraville
770-986-0032
elreydeltacoatl.com

While Martin suggests eating the Camaron "El Rey" Delicioso (shrimp) Taco the way it comes, for the Pulpo Encebollado (octopus grilled with onions), he suggests adding green salsa, a dash of red salsa, and a squeeze of lime, and stuffing the Pescado (fish) Taco with the salad, pico de gallo, and green salsa.

EMERALD CITY BAGELS

The wizards of New York–style bagels

"One Saturday I was bored, so I decided to see if I could make bagels," recalls Deanna Halcrow. She's loved to cook since she was a teenager; and as a New Yorker living in Atlanta, she'd never found bagels that met her standards. Her first batch wasn't great, but she kept experimenting. Soon, Deanna was pawning off bagels on family and neighbors.

Meanwhile, her daughter, Jackie, was miserable in her job. Jackie had attended culinary school and worked in restaurants, but for the past 10 years had been working in retail. Mother and daughter began toying with the idea of selling bagels.

On Mother's Day 2012, they brought samples to a friend who co-owned Argosy in East Atlanta. He was impressed and said he'd buy their bagels once they were cooking in a commercial kitchen. "That was the first time we thought 'maybe we can do this,'" remembers Jackie. They were one of the first tenants to sign up for Prep, a shared kitchen in Chamblee.

From the start, their wholesale business kept them afloat, but their Sunday pop-ups built their retail customer base. They set up a folding table in the courtyard of Deanna's Cabbagetown condo building and sold to neighbors. As word spread, they moved out of the gated community, relocating in front of businesses on Carroll Street.

Jackie and Deanna had always been close, but soon they were working together almost every day. Deanna learned to set aside her

For the freshest bagels, arrive as early as 6 a.m., when you can watch them being made! You won't find any day-old bagels here! Bagels that don't sell are either donated to local nonprofits or turned into bagel chips.

Top left: All bagels are baked fresh, in house, each morning. *Above left:* Whitefish salad with dill cream cheese and red caviar on an onion bagel. *Top right:* What's more classic than bagel and lox? *Above right:* On weekends, customers line up outside to get their bagel fix. All photos by David Parham.

role as "mom" when they're at work. For Jackie, the strangest part was learning to call her mom by her first name. "When we hired our first employee, I thought, 'I guess I have to start calling her Deanna now.'"

In January 2018, they opened their first brick-and-mortar location in East Atlanta Village, where they now produce bagels for both the shop and wholesale. Originally, they didn't have a toaster, which became a point of contention on a neighborhood Facebook page. "Bagelgate" ended when Deanna and Jackie conceded and purchased a toaster, but they still have strong feelings on the subject.

"A bagel should never be toasted," Jackie says firmly. "it's a fresh bread. We have the bagel come out of the oven as it's meant to be consumed. And it just tastes better. If you slice it and toast it, you pull out the moisture and change the texture. You're not actually enjoying the product the way we intended."

1257-A Glenwood Ave. SE
404-343-3758
emeraldcitybagels.com

ATLANTA CHINATOWN MALL

The best food court you've never heard of

Across the globe, many major cities have a Chinatown—an ethnic enclave of Chinese people who have emigrated from mainland China or Hong Kong.

Atlanta has a Chinatown, too. Well, sort of. . . .

Atlanta Chinatown Mall in Chamblee offers a variety of specialty stores, a supermarket, and one of the best food courts in Atlanta. Built in 1988, the mall is anchored by Dinho Supermarket (an Asian grocery store), Oriental Pearl (a dim sum restaurant with huge tables perfect for large parties), and El Caballo Dorado Golden Saloon (a Mexican bar/restaurant).

In the back corner is one of the most underrated food courts in the city. The original plan was for each vendor to represent a different region of China. When it first opened, all the menus were in Mandarin. Over the years, both the vendors and the customer base have changed. Now all the menus (most of which include more than 100 dishes) are in English as well as Mandarin.

You won't find any fast-food chains in the food court. Each stall is a mom-and-pop restaurant that cooks dishes from scratch. You'll find restaurant-quality dishes at food-court prices.

Stop by New Lan Zhoa Noodle to watch Chef Shufeng Guo pull noodles by hand, the way he learned living in northeast China. In addition to ordering a bowl of noodle soup, you won't want to miss his dumplings.

Each year, the mall hosts a free Lunar New Year celebration with music, dance performances, and, of course, great food.

Left: A bowl of soup from Chong Qing Hot Pot can easily serve four. Photo by George Gussin. *Center:* Hong Kong BBQ is the spot for roast duck. Photo by George Gussin. *Top right:* Relax with a pot of oolong tea from Maomi Bookstore. Photo courtesy of Maomi Bookstore. *Above right:* Family Baking makes custom cakes, even a durian cake! Photo courtesy of Family Baking.

Chong Qing Hot Pot still serves their namesake steaming bowls of soup brought to the table with a portable burner to keep them warm, but it's the spicy Szechuan dishes the new owner, Chef Liang, is really known for. Try Chong Qing Spicy Chicken, Eggplant with Garlic Sauce, and Dry Fish Hot Pot.

Hong Kong BBQ is easy to spot, with its window full of hanging roast ducks. Deservedly known for their roast duck, pork, and chicken, the restaurant also sports an extensive Cantonese menu.

For less-adventurous eaters, Top One Gourmet, China Kitchen, and Yanmi Yanmi offer Americanized dishes such as Sweet and Sour Chicken, General Tso's Chicken, and chicken wings, in addition to more authentic dishes.

For a sweet treat, Family Baking bakes popular pastries from Hong Kong, Taiwan, and Malaysia, including mini Swiss rolls, egg tarts, and sweet buns. The bakery specializes in custom cakes and vegan desserts.

Finish your visit with a cup of tea at Maomi Bookstore, where you can browse stationery, imported books, specialty food items, and tea.

5383 New Peachtree Rd., Chamblee
770-458-6660

The best seats in the house are just outside the food court in the courtyard garden, complete with a koi pond and a mural of the Great Wall of China.

SOUL VEGETARIAN

Pioneering the Black vegan movement

Fried chicken, mac 'n' cheese, collards stewed in with a ham hock—soul food takes many forms, but you have to look far and wide to find vegan versions. Fortunately for Atlanta's vegans, there's Soul Veg.

Soul Vegetarian, opened in 1979 by the Hebrew Israelite Community of Jerusalem, offers a wide array of vegan comfort food and fresh juices. Also known by such names as the Black Hebrew Israelites, the Black Hebrews, or Black Israelites, members believe that the key to healthy living can be found in Scripture:

"And God said, 'Behold, I have given you every herb bearing seed, which is upon the face of all the Earth and every tree in which is the fruit of a tree yielding seed. To you it shall be for food.'"— Genesis 1:29

The Black Hebrews interpret this verse to mean that a healthy diet includes only foods with seeds, leading them to follow a vegan diet.

At the height of the movement, there were more than 25,000 Hebrew Israelites in the US. They operated their own restaurants in Chicago, Tallahassee, Cleveland, St. Louis, Atlanta, and Washington, DC. Over the years, many have closed, but both Atlanta locations, with their unique reinterpretation of Southern soul food, remain.

Sides (mac 'n' cheese, collard greens, corn on the cob, baked potato, sweet potatoes, potato salad, broccoli, brown rice with gravy, and cornbread) are soul food staples, but the entrees (Cauliflower, Tofu, and Kalebone Twists) are uniquely Soul Veg.

You won't find Impossible Burgers or other mass-produced meat alternatives here. Everything is made in-house, from the Garvey Burger (named for the Black-nationalist leader, Marcus Garvey) to the Kalebone (a homemade meat alternative made from the gluten in wheat flour). Each day, they offer a half-dozen or more fresh salads, including the Eggless Salad and the inexplicably addictive Carrot Salad.

Top left: Soul Vegetarian #1 and #2 (pictured) serve vegan versions of soul food favorites. Photo by Adrienne Bruce. *Above left:* The Country Baked Steak is seasoned kalebone battered, baked, and smothered with a rich brown gravy, and served here with vegan mac 'n' cheese and collard greens. *Top right:* The Garvey Burger is named for the Black-nationalist leader Marcus Garvey, and is served with herb-roasted potatoes. *Above right:* The vegan "Ice Kream" (made with a coconut and soy base) and the Royal Ginger Root (a refreshing drink of pineapple juice, fresh ginger, lemon juice, and honey) can be purchased to-go. Photo by Adrienne Bruce.

For a tangy, refreshing drink, order the Royal Ginger Root, made with pineapple juice, fresh ginger, lemon juice, honey, and water.

For dessert, vegans and nonvegans alike can't resist a scoop of Soul Veg's coconut- and soy-based "Ice Kream." Pints are available to take home.

Today, there are approximately 5,000 Hebrew Israelites around the world. Most live in Israel, but the 75 who call Atlanta home continue to provide homemade vegan soul food at locations in the West End and Poncey Highlands.

West End:
879 Ralph David Abernathy Blvd. SW
404-752-5194

Poncey-Highland:
652 N. Highland Ave.
404-875-0145

soulvegsouth.com

Order a dish of seaweed to go along with your Carrot Salad; you'll swear you were eating tuna salad.

A cup of confidence

In 2017, the City of Alpharetta held a series of listening sessions and asked residents, "How do we make Alpharetta the best place to live in Georgia?" For one thing, they were told, the city lacked programs for people with developmental and intellectual disabilities.

People with intellectual disabilities can excel in suitable work environments, especially if given appropriate training and guidance. However, nationally their unemployment rate is 83 percent. All too often, employers don't want to hire someone who is "different." And sometimes when they do, they fail to make needed accommodations.

That's what happened to Griffin Rudd.

Griffin was hired as a cashier at his favorite fast-food restaurant. At the end of one shift, his drawer was $5 short. His boss told him to slow down so he wouldn't make mistakes because if it happened again, he'd be fired. Griffin was afraid, so he deliberately slowed down to make sure he didn't mess up again. Unfortunately, he was fired for being too slow. Griffin felt like he couldn't do anything right.

It wasn't that Griffin couldn't do the job; he just needed a manager who took time to understand that he takes instructions literally, so he needs clearly stated directions.

After the city donated space in the Alpharetta Community Center for a job-training program, a volunteer planning group decided a café was just the ticket. Parents regularly drop off kids for dance class and basketball practice, so a café would be an ideal place for them to wait. Also, a café provided the opportunity for employees to practice several teachable skills: making coffee, operating the cash register, and serving customers. Each shift, a brewista partners with a manager for one-on-one support.

Left: Start your day with a warm latte and an even warmer smile. *Top center:* The Café Intermezzo team taught the brewistas to make cake pops from leftover cake tops. *Above center:* Brewistas learn valuable skills from using a cash register to helping customers. *Right:* Pups are not only welcome but also spoiled with a Pup Cup!

In six months as a brewista, Griffin regained needed self-confidence.

"Working at BrewAble changed Griffin," says Nicky Rudd, Griffin's mom and board president of BrewAble, the nonprofit café. "Everyone knew him, and he was treated like a rock star. Now, in his new job, he knows how to advocate for himself and how to ask for help."

Café Intermezzo (see page 148) donates cake tops for the brewistas to transform into colorful cake pops. The coffee is roasted by an Alpharetta-based roaster, and the scones are from Seven Sisters Kitchen in Johns Creek. The café also sells artwork by local artists with developmental disabilities.

You'll walk away from BrewAble Café with a warm feeling, and it won't be just from the coffee.

175 Roswell St., Alpharetta
brewablecafe.com

BrewAble is a great place for a date with your dog. Not only are there walking trails and a dog park in adjacent Wills Park, but you also can bring your dog inside the cafe for a Pup Cup, a cup of whipped cream that is sure to get her tail wagging!

Tex-Mex meets dive bar

Like many of his contemporaries in their teens and 20s, Alex Skalicky bounced around different restaurants across Atlanta. In 1991, he found himself working at Tortillas, the hub of indie culture.

Working alongside DJs, graffiti artists, and musicians, he fell in love with mission-style burritos. Owner Charlie Kerns taught him the value of simplicity, cooking most dishes with just five spices: salt, garlic, pepper, chili, and cumin.

When his friend Skip Sinanian opened the Righteous Room, it was a revelation for Alex that bars could serve really good food. Eventually, the two of them set out to create a bar, "where you can raise hell and eat great Mexican food." (Skip's no longer with Elmyr; Jim Shelly is now co-owner.)

The restaurant is named after a notorious Hungarian artist, Elmyr de Hory, with whom Alex became fascinated while doing research for a college class.

De Hory made little money selling his own work but found a more lucrative vocation as an art forger. He began doing knockoffs of paintings by noted artists for knowing customers. Then he hooked up with an art dealer to create forgeries and sell them as originals. To this day, de Hory is considered one of the greatest art forgers of all time; no one knows how many of his works hang in museums.

The art forger is an appropriate namesake for a Mexican joint run by a bunch of white guys. To pay homage to de Hory, friends of the owners painted replicas of famous paintings for Elmyr. And over the

> Not into the bar scene? You'll find many of the same dishes at Elmyr's family-friendly sister restaurant, Elmyriachi, in Kirkwood.

Left: Elmyr owners Alex Skalicky and Jim Shelly. *Center:* Elmyr's quesadillas and Mission-style burritos are packed full of fresh ingredients. *Right:* Elmyr is a cross between a dive bar and a burrito joint.

jukebox hangs a painting of their No. 1 customer, Darren, drinking with the notorious art forger.

While the celebrity headshots on display are genuine, some signatures are suspect.

Elmyr burritos are stuffed with whole beans and fresh vegetables. Some house burritos (the Nacho Burrito, Brunswick Stew Burrito, and the Pad Thai Burrito) started out as playful experiments for their recession special—a beer and a Burrito of the Day for $5. Others (hot dog burrito, anyone?) did not make the cut.

In the "dranks" section of the menu, below the margaritas and the other Mexican-inspired cocktails, you'll find Elmyr's signature drink: the Grizz. This Mexican Car Bomb is simply a bottle of Coronita (a baby Corona), topped off with a shot of tequila. This best seller is so popular that more than one person is walking around this planet with a Grizz tattoo.

Elmyr
1091 Euclid Ave. NE
404-588-0250
elmyr.com

Elmyriachi
1950 Hosea L. Williams Dr. NE
678-705-9902
elmyriachi.com

KIMBALL HOUSE & WATCHMAN'S

A hotel bar without a hotel

What happens when two pairs of friends collide while working in the restaurant industry? They start dreaming up their own restaurant concept.

That's what happened when Matt Christison and Miles Macquarrie met Bryan Rackley and Jesse Smith while all of them worked at the Brick Store Pub in Decatur. The four saw restaurants as a way to introduce the community to new flavors and ingredients.

But before they could educate customers, they had to educate themselves. While they all had come of age working in restaurants, none was a classically trained chef. To compensate for their lack of training, they made it their mission to study menus whenever they traveled.

On a trip to Tampa, Bryan dined at legendary Bern's Steakhouse, where he was inspired by the extensive caviar menu. He texted the menu to the others, who agreed their menu should feature a caviar section. After all, their restaurant was to be a grand experiment. They'd try things out and see how the dining community responds.

And respond they did. In 2013, Kimball House opened in an 1891 freight depot owned by the City of Decatur. A series of restaurants that had occupied the space previously had failed. Kimball House has broken the curse.

Aspiring to evoke a classic hotel bar vibe, they researched historical hotel lounge menus. They learned that a cornerstone dish was the three-course Steak Dinner, which is why it shares permanent billing at the Kimball House with such classics as Beef Tartare, Shrimp Cocktail, and Chicken-Liver Mousse.

Left: Watchman's happy hour is a must for oyster lovers. *Center:* Kimball House partners Bryan Rackley, Matt Christison, Jesse Smith, and Miles Macquarrie. *Right:* The classic Steak Dinner, with a soup, salad, and choice of cut, is a menu staple.

But the two items everyone comes to Kimball House for are the cocktails and the oysters. Miles is a genius behind the bar and has developed one of the most celebrated beverage programs in the city.

Oysters have been on the menu since day one. Initially, the shellfish came from the northeast and the northwest—southern oysters were noticeably absent. Bryan, who has a passion for promoting sustainable aquaculture, cofounded Oyster South, a nonprofit that advocates for the southern oyster-farming industry. This helps ensure that Kimball House can shuck fresh oysters and support the environment and regional aquaculture at the same time.

If Kimball House is out of your price range, check out the more casual spinoff Watchman in Krog Street Market. The cocktails and oysters are just as good, and the menu focuses on southern seafood and shellfish.

Kimball House
303 E. Howard Ave., Decatur
404-254-0141
kimball-house.com

Watchman's
99 Krog St. NE
404-254-0141
watchmansatl.com

Regulars know to order Caviar and Middlins with a side of chicken skins, for dipping in the bowl of creamy white grits, topped with a soft poached egg and white sturgeon caviar.

SWEET HUT & FOOD TERMINAL

Enough is not enough

When she was an accountant in Malaysia, Amy Wong and her three daughters sold bread at the morning market to make ends meet. As part of the informal economy, they would run and hide their goods when someone yelled "Police!"

In a country with limited economic opportunities, you do what you can to get by, which is why the family immigrated to the US in 1999. Amy and her brother-in-law, Howie Ewe, partnered with two others to open Top Spice, a Thai and Malaysian restaurant in Toco Hills.

But it was Amy's husband, Patrick Ewe, who had the vision for Sweet Hut, an Asian bakery where people of all ages could hang out all day—where parents could bring their children in the mornings, business people could stop in for lunch, and high school kids could hang out past midnight.

With more than 200 items on the menu, there's something for everyone. Customers use tongs to fill their plastic trays with an assortment of Asian baked goods: Cantonese BBQ pork buns, Portuguese egg tarts, pillowy Hokkaido cupcakes from Japan, soft and sweet Taiwanese bread, and neon green pandan cupcakes from Malaysia.

Of the 100 drink options, Sweet Hut is best known for their milk teas (bubble teas). The 12 types of tea (including taro, coconut, hazelnut, and honey jasmine green) can be customized with toppings ranging from the popular boba (soaked in honey and brown sugar for a caramel taste) to more adventurous options (aloe vera jelly cubes,

> When ordering your boba tea, you can ask for less (or more) sweetness.

Top left: Sweet Hut founders Patrick Ewe and Amy Wong. *Above left:* Mooncakes are traditionally given to friends and family members during the Mid-Autumn Festival in China. Sweet Hut bakes a number of flavors, including the traditional lotus and red-bean filled with a salted duck egg. *Center:* Taro Milk Tea with tapioca bubbles and a Matcha Donut. *Right:* Sample popular Malaysian street food dishes at Food Terminal.

custard pudding, grass jelly, or popping boba—thin filaments filled with flavor that pop in your mouth).

Buford Highway was certainly ready for Sweet Hut. With a grand opening banner as their only marketing tool, the bakery sold out within hours, forcing them to close the following day to restock. Today, there are six Sweet Hut locations around Atlanta.

The Ewes were so impressed by locals' willingness to try new items that they recently opened Food Terminal, a sit-down restaurant specializing in Malaysian street food. Once again, the opening day response was overwhelming, and they had to close after two days to restock. Clearly, Atlanta was ready for Food Terminal, too.

Photos in the more than 30-page menu can stir up FOMO. Best to stick to favorites such as Curry Noodle Soup, Penang Prawn Ree, Hainanese Chicken Rice, and Grandma's BBQ Pork–Tossed Noodles.

Sweet Hut
Various locations
www.sweethutbakery.com

Food Terminal

Chamblee:
5000 Buford Hwy. B201
678-353-6110

West Midtown:
1000 Marietta St., NW #202
678-400-8155

foodterminal.com

Polenta party: no plates needed

Ernest Hemingway described the blank page as "the white bull." While the sensation can strike fear in a writer's heart, for Chef Pat Pascarella, the name speaks of endless possibility.

For a first-generation Italian American who makes pasta from scratch, opening an Italian restaurant might have been a logical move. But Pat didn't want to box himself in, preferring to let his mood on a given day determine what he would cook. Each morning a clean slate. Each daily menu a blank page. Ergo, the White Bull.

For a unique dining experience, grab five (or more) of your closest friends and make reservations for a Polenta Party at White Bull or its sister location, Grana in Piedmont Heights. Inspired by a dinner Pat's aunt hosted in Italy, guests are treated to a set-price, three-course dinner. Each meal opens with a seasonal salad and individual loaves of *sfincione*, a bread made from a Sicilian-style pizza dough.

Next comes the main event. White Bull chefs make their polenta by milling the cornmeal in-house, then adding butter, cheese, mascarpone, and cream to make a rich porridge. Chef Pascarella covers the table with butcher paper before pouring a pot of creamy polenta down the middle. Heaping servings of meats and seasonal vegetables are piled on the polenta and topped with olive oil and freshly grated parmesan cheese.

Guests eat right off the butcher paper. Why dirty dishes when you can eat right off the table?

For those who still have room, the final course is a house-made dessert, which, like most of the selections, changes frequently. You may be treated to an individual cheesecake, a slice of tres leches cake, or a build-your-own cannoli bar.

The farm-to-table menu changes daily, but the homemade pastas are always the center of attention. Depending on the season, you

Top left: White Bull's Polenta Party is as Instagram-worthy as it is delicious. *Above left:* Mascarpone cheese is folded into the pasta at the end to give a little touch of richness to the Pappardelle Bolognese. *Right:* As the name suggests, Spaghetti Cacio e Pepe pairs black pepper with grated Pecorino Romano cheese.

may find black spaghetti served with shrimp, sausage, jalapeños, and tomato; or *garganelli* (a cylindrical shaped egg-based pasta) with prosciutto, black truffle, and *piave* (an Italian cow's milk cheese).

If you can't decide what to order, reserve a spot for the Chef's Tasting. The five-course tasting menu features the freshest ingredients from local purveyors. Guests can add on a flight of homemade pasta and wine pairings.

In 2020, Chef Pat opened Grana, specializing in Neapolitan pizza, handmade pasta, wood-fired steaks, and meatball flights

So whether you're looking for some homemade pasta or a one-of-a-kind polenta party, just head to Decatur to take this bull by the horns.

<table>
<tr><td>The White Bull</td><td>Grana</td></tr>
<tr><td>123 E. Court Square, Decatur</td><td>1835 Piedmont Ave.</td></tr>
<tr><td>404-600-5649</td><td>404-231-9000</td></tr>
<tr><td>whitebullatl.com</td><td>granaatl.com</td></tr>
</table>

Check the website for upcoming farm tours and classes such as pasta-making, bread-making, and cocktail mixing.

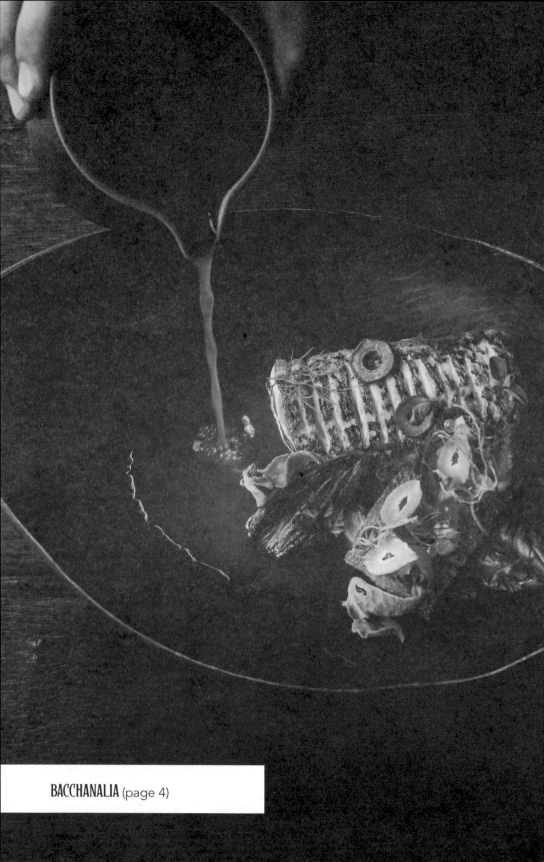

BACCHANALIA (page 4)

TICONDEROGA CLUB (page 152)

DUTCH MONKEY DOUGNUTS (page 12)

THE TAMARIND GROUP (page 36)

FOOD TERMINAL (page 80)

SWEET AUBURN BBQ (page 106)

TWISTED SOUL COOKHOUSE & POURS (page 114)

TALAT MARKET (page 128)

BREWABLE CAFÉ (page 74)

EL BURRO POLLO (page 130)

SNACKBOXE BISTRO (page 142)

THE VARSITY (page 24)

FROSTY CABOOSE (page 182)

SUSHI HAYAKAWA (page 58)

YOUR DEKALB FARMERS MARKET (page 112)

DELIA'S CHICKEN SAUSAGE STAND (page 164)

MILLER UNION (page 32)

PATEL PLAZA

Atlanta's Little India

A number of Indian restaurants are scattered throughout North Decatur, but nowhere is there a higher concentration than at Patel Plaza. Southeast Asian families trek across the state to shop and eat at this strip mall. Anchored by Patel Brothers, an Indian grocery store with more than 50 locations in the United States, the plaza is home to sari boutiques, jewelry stores, spas, and almost a dozen restaurants.

At first glance, the menu at Chinese Dhaba looks familiar, with Chinese favorites such as fried rice, spring rolls, and lo mein. But a closer look reveals an Indian twist. Their signature dish, Chicken Bullet, consists of fried pieces of boneless chicken marinated in a spicy sauce with Indian flavors. The Paneer Manchurian pairs the Indian cheese with onions, cilantro, and a house-made Indochinese sauce (chinesedhaba.com).

Masala offers North Indian cuisine in a more upscale atmosphere, including a full bar. Before the pandemic, Masala was best known for its buffet. The menu is extensive, with more than 100 options, from Chicken Tikka to Catfish Masala (masaladecatur.com).

The newest spot to join the plaza is Roti n' Grill. The modest menu offers such grilled items as Tava Lamb Chops (grilled lamb served with a spicy tomato, onion, and chili sauce) and Indian-inspired burgers and sliders (rotingrill.com).

As its name suggests, Thali specializes in *thali*, a meal made up of several small dishes served together on a platter. Each thali includes three vegetarian dishes, *dahl* (a thick lentil soup), rice, *roti* (an Indian flatbread), and pickles. Tucked away inside Patel Plaza, Thali offers cozy booths with plump, saffron cushions (eatatthali.com).

Originally a family-run street cart in Ahmedabad, India, Honest Restaurant is now an international franchise offering vegetarian

Chicken 65, a spicy, deep-fried Indochinese chicken dish, at Chinese Dhaba.

street foods, cooked to order. The Bhaji Pav is a thick curry made from fresh vegetables, spices, and a special butter imported from India, served with fluffy, buttery rolls—perfect for dunking in the stew. The Bahubali sandwich resembles a club sandwich filled with fresh vegetables, a green chili sauce, and a sweet tomato sauce topped with cheese (honestrestaurantsusa.com).

Chat Patti pulls inspiration straight from the streets of Ahmedabad, India. Khiladi Special Sandwich, Hot Dog Veg Ahmedabad Special, and Manek Chowk Indian-Style Pizza replicate trendy street food dishes. The menu also sports *chaat* (a savory snack loaded with sauces and toppings), Indo-Chinese, South Indian, and Punjab dishes. The Special Chaat is a plate full of flat flour crisps (similar to dry cereal), topped high with chickpeas, lentil doughnuts, onions, yogurt, tamarind sauce, a green chutney, and more (chatpattiatl.com).

Gokul serves vegetarian dishes from across India, including *dhosas* (thin rice pancakes that resemble a crepe) from South India and a popular Indochinese section. There's also a huge display of sweets, savory snacks, and homemade *kulfi* (ice cream) pops in mango, *pista* (pistachio), *kesar pista* (saffron pistachio), and *mall* (milk) flavors. Order the popular street snack *panipuri*, a fried puff filled with chutneys, vegetables, and flavored water, which you pop into your mouth for a single bite (gokulsweets.com).

Georgia Halal Meat is primarily a butcher shop, offering custom cuts of locally sourced goat and chicken. There's no seating inside, but their full kitchen prepares a number of goat, chicken, and vegetarian dishes to go. Try a whole tandoori chicken.

The first thing you notice walking into Royal Sweets is a bright orange food truck parked right in the dining room. The next thing to catch your eye is a display case full of colorful Indian *mithai* (sweets), including *burfee*, *halwa*, *peda*, *ladoo*, and *kaju*. Don't let the name fool you; savory dishes such as *samosas* (deep-fried pastries with potatoes and peas) and African Chaat (a savory snack mix with a kick) are not to be missed. Everything, including the Indian-inspired ice creams, is made locally (royalsweetsatlanta.com).

Bawatchi Biryanis specializes in—you guessed it—*biryanis*, a mixed rice dish originating in the Muslim areas of India. In this aromatic dish, basmati rice is cooked with marinated meat (chicken, goat, or shrimp), egg, *paneer* (cheese), or vegetables and spices, and then served with *mirchi ka salan* (curried chilli peppers) and *raita* (yogurt mixed with chopped vegetables) (bawarchidecatur.com).

Upstairs, Blueberry's Raju Omlet Centre offers two menus. Blueberry's serves Punjabi dishes, while the Raju Omelette Centre menu is based on a popular roadside cafeteria in India that serves only egg dishes. The Raju Chef Special brings together three egg preparations (omelette, sunny-side up, and hard boiled) with a tasty sauce and lots of melted cheese (rajuomletcentre.com).

Patel Plaza
1709 Church St.

Top left: Honest Restaurant's Bhaji Pav, a thick curry made from fresh vegetables, spices, and a special butter imported from India, served with fluffy, buttery rolls. *Above:* An assortment of desserts from Royal Sweets. Photo by Mathilde Piard. *Top right:* Goat Biryani from Bawatchi Biryanis.

North Decatur is full of Indian restaurants and stores, including Zyka (1677 Scott Blvd., Zyka.com), the vegetarian Madras Mantra (2179 Lawrenceville Hwy., 404-636-4400, madrasmantra.com), and Cherians International Groceries (751 Dekalb Industrial Way, Building #4, cherians.com).

SWEET AUBURN BARBECUE

BBQ with an Asian twang

The food industry is a common landing place for many immigrants, as an opportunity to work hard and build a better life for their children.

When Betty and George Hsu emigrated from Malaysia, they worked in restaurant kitchens before opening Hunan Village, which they would grow into their own chain of Chinese restaurants in the Atlanta area. Like most newcomers, their goal was for their children to be able to follow any career path they chose.

After growing up in the family restaurants, the next generation of Hsus were eager to pursue careers outside of hospitality. Howard worked for an import/export company, Anita went to school for medicine, and Ron (see page 108) studied business.

By her senior year in college, Anita concluded that medicine wasn't for her. Until she could settle on her next career move, she decided she would temporarily do what she already knew. She and Howard opened Gezzo's West Coast Burritos in a strip mall in Henry County.

When the owner of a neighboring CiCi's Pizza franchise, Dave Buster, bought a smoker and concessions trailer, he and Howard began swapping recipes and marketing ideas. Before long, Anita and Howard were partners with Dave, spending weekends slinging BBQ at festivals around town.

After selling outside of the Municipal Market (better known as the Sweet Auburn Curb Market) for several weeks, they secured a stall inside and launched their permanent business, Sweet Auburn Barbecue.

When it comes to BBQ, everyone's first question is "What style is it?"

"We're creating an Atlanta-style BBQ," says Anita. "Atlanta's a melting pot, and our BBQ is a little bit of the different cultures."

The Hsus blend their Malay and Chinese heritage with their Southern upbringing in such dishes as Pimento Cheese Wontons,

Left: Handmade Pimento Cheese Wontons. *Center:* The Hsu Siblings—Howard, Anita, and Ron—in front of Sweet Auburn BBQ. *Right:* Sweet and Spicy BBQ Wu Tang Wings. All photos by Madelyn Turner.

served with a sweet Thai chili sauce. The popular Wu Tang Wings pair a BBQ rub with sweet chili sauce in a five-step process in which the wings are brined, seasoned, smoked, and fried before being tossed with the sauce.

Their second location, on Highland Avenue, is a full-service restaurant featuring a bar where the smoke isn't limited to the food. For the Don't Burn Down the House, a cocktail glass is inverted over a chunk of smoking hickory wood before being filled with a concoction of bourbon, maple syrup, black walnut bitters, and Creole bitters. A more fitting cocktail for a BBQ restaurant you'll be hard-pressed to find.

656 North Highland Ave.
678-515-3550

Curb Market, 209 Edgewood Ave. SE
404-589-9722

sweetauburnbbq.com

> The most popular dish is the BBQ Taco (choice of pulled chicken, pulled pork, or brisket). It's topped with slaw, pickles, and BBQ sauce on a flour tortilla. For vegetarians, both locations offer a veggie plate. Also, the Highland location offers BBQ-Rubbed Tofu.

LAZY BETTY

Let the chef order for you

The Hsu family is a culinary institution in Atlanta. Parents Betty and George opened the first Chinese restaurant in Henry County—Hunan Village in Stockbridge—and then proceeded to open locations in Griffin, McDonough, Ellenwood, and Locust Grove.

Having grown up spending every afternoon after school, weekends, and summer vacation helping out at the restaurant, Ron—and his siblings, Anita and Howard (see page 106)—envisioned futures for themselves outside of the food industry.

Ron studied business at UGA, but, a few years in, decided he'd rather be cooking. Betty was supportive, encouraging him to drop out of UGA and enroll in Le Cordon Bleu Australia.

After a stint at Dish in Virginia Highlands, Ron moved to New York City, where he worked his way up from *stagiaire* (an apprentice who works for free) to creative director at the three-Michelin-Star Le Bernardin.

Ten years later, Ron returned to Atlanta to be closer to family and open his first restaurant. He teamed up with fellow Le Bernardin alum Aaron Phillips to create Lazy Betty, a rare tasting-menu-only restaurant in the city.

The duo strive to push forward Atlanta's culinary scene by offering NYC-quality, high-end dining in an unpretentious atmosphere. With neither dress code nor white tablecloths, Lazy Betty reimagines "dining fine" as an approachable, welcoming experience.

The name is a cheeky nod to Ron's mom, who was anything but lazy. One night, Betty was babysitting Anita's kids while she picked

Instead of tipping, a service fee is included in the price, allowing the restaurant to pay the staff a living wage.

Top left: Charred Spanish octopus, fermented black bean, and Pearson peaches. *Above left:* The simple, elegant interior of Lazy Betty. *Center:* Le Bernardin alum Aaron Phillips and Ron Hsu came together to create Lazy Betty. *Right:* Foie Gras with petite salad and gooseberry center. All photos by Madelyn Turner.

up Ron from the airport. Returning home after 1 a.m. to find their mother asleep on the couch surrounded by laundry, Anita quipped, "That's our mom, 'Lazy Betty.'" The name stuck. It had the playful, unpretentious vibe Ron was looking for.

Guests select from a four-, seven-, or ten-course tasting menu for a curated dining experience, which takes between two and three hours. Ron creates dishes that combine his family's Chinese and Malay roots with his own Southern upbringing, as well as French techniques he learned in culinary school and honed at Le Bernardin.

Ron orchestrates an emotional or intellectual twist on each plate. His Grilled Spanish Octopus with paprika, preserved lemon, and pimenton (smoked paprika) is paired with French-style sauce made with Chinese fermented black beans. These ingredients shouldn't go together, yet they do.

In 2019, Lazy Betty was recognized as the best new restaurant by *Atlanta Magazine*, Thrillist, and Eater Atlanta. It was named a James Beard Award semifinalist for Best New Restaurant the following year.

1530 DeKalb Ave. NE
404-975-3692
lazybettyatl.com

Serving those who serve us

While there are thousands of restaurants in the Atlanta area that serve us, there's only one nonprofit whose mission is to support the food service workers who serve us.

The late Chef Ryan Hidinger honed his culinary skills under Anne Quatrano at Bacchanalia (see page 4) before taking a position at Muss & Turner's in Smyrna to learn the business side. His goal was to open Staplehouse, where he'd cook side by side with fellow chef and close friend Ryan Smith.

To develop the Staplehouse concept, Ryan and his wife, Jen, started Prelude to Staplehouse, a weekly, underground dinner series in their home. As word of their dinners began to spread, soon every dinner sold out almost as soon as it was announced.

For four years, Ryan and Jen worked full time, while hosting dinners on Sundays and developing their business plan for Staplehouse. Finally, in the summer of 2012, they lined up financing and found a space for their restaurant. Before year's end, however, an MRI showed that what Ryan suspected was a bout of flu was actually liver cancer. On the verge of realizing his dream, Ryan Hidinger was given six months to live.

His mentors at Muss & Turner's, Ryan Turner, Todd Mussman, and Chris Hall, organized a fundraiser for the couple. They hoped to raise $25,000 with Team Hidi, where guests sampled dishes from Atlanta restaurants and bid at a live auction. They raised $250,000!

Within days, they were laying the framework for Giving Kitchen, a nonprofit that provides emergency assistance to food service workers through financial support and a network of community resources.

Food service workers experiencing a housing emergency or needing to miss work due to injury, illness, or loss of a loved one can receive financial assistance. Giving Kitchen also connects workers to

Top left: Giving Kitchen Executive Director Bryan Schroeder joins cofounders Jen Hidinger-Kendrick and Ryan Turner in accepting the James Beard Foundation's 2019 Humanitarian of the Year award. *Above left:* For food service workers in moments of crisis, Giving Kitchen staff and volunteers are heroes. Photo by Erika Botfeld. *Right:* With many of the best chefs volunteering their talents, Giving Kitchen fundraisers are always tasty!

a network of stability partners and community resources, including doctors, mental health providers, and housing specialists.

Ryan died in 2014. The following year, Jen, Ryan Smith, and Kara Hidinger (Ryan Hidinger's sister, married to Ryan Smith), opened Staplehouse. Originally a high-end, tasting-menu experience owned by Giving Kitchen, in 2020, Ryan and Kara purchased Staplehouse and transformed it into a neighborhood market offering prepared foods.

Over the years, Giving Kitchen's mission has expanded to include food service workers in fast-food eateries, catering, coffee shops, concessions, and even food trucks across Georgia. In 2019, Giving Kitchen was named Humanitarian of the Year by the James Beard Foundation.

givingkitchen.org

Visit the Events Calendar at givingkitchen.org for details about some tasty fundraisers!

YOUR DEKALB FARMERS MARKET

A world market

Whatever you think when you hear "farmers market," toss it out the window. Your Dekalb Farmers Market (YDFM) is unlike any place you've been before.

Robert Blazer grew up in his father's discount store in Rhode Island. When he was six, he accompanied his dad to trade shows, consulting on which toys the store should carry. Retail is in his blood.

Following engineering school, Robert continued to work for his father, but the two often butted heads. Once, when his father was out of town, Robert stocked onions and potatoes in the basement. His father was furious; they weren't in the perishables business.

But that was the business Robert wanted to be in. So he moved to Atlanta, where his sister lived, and hired neighborhood kids to help him build a small structure in Decatur. With the last of his money, he bought a load of produce from the Atlanta Curb Market. If it didn't sell, that would be it for him.

Turns out, it was just the beginning.

Robert began purchasing directly from farmers. Skipping the middle man had two advantages: produce was cheaper, and it had a longer shelf-life. Without refrigeration, however, his store was open Thursday through Sunday only, and unsold produce was auctioned-off Sunday evening.

After 10 years, the market had succeeded to the point where Robert was able to buy land in Decatur and build a 140,000-square-foot warehouse.

The market has evolved along with its customers. YDFM still purchases produce directly from local farmers, but they also buy

Left: The seafood department offers more than 450 varieties of whole fish, fillets, and shellfish. *Center:* The aisles get crowded during the weekends, so shop during the week if you can. *Right:* An array of baked goods are made in-house with no artificial ingredients or preservatives.

produce from all over the US and abroad. Today YDFM reflects its diverse clientele, including immigrants and refugees, who have flocked to the Atlanta region in recent years. Customers from countries as distant and diverse as Cambodia and Ethiopia know they can find the ingredients they miss from back home. Staffers represent 40-some countries and speak more than 50 languages.

The market offers more than fruits and vegetables. There are extensive selections of seafood, meat, and dairy; fresh ground nut butters and coffees; every dried herb and spice imaginable; beautiful flowers; wines and beers from around the world; and dry goods. YDFM also offers its own line of food, including pastas, pizza, sausages, and smoked meats. The pastry shop will satisfy any sweet tooth, and the bakery offers an array of baked goods made in-house with no artificial ingredients or preservatives.

3000 E. Ponce de Leon Ave.
404-377-6400
dekalbfarmersmarket.com

YDFM is chilly. It's always 62 degrees inside to help preserve the produce. Wear a warm layer. The aisles can get crowded but are easier to navigate with one of the small red plastic carts by the front entrances. If you're anticipating a big load, pick up one of the larger carts from the parking lot because you won't find one near the entrance. Credit cards are not accepted.

TWISTED SOUL COOKHOUSE & POURS

From turbulence to tasty

For Deborah VanTrece, becoming a flight attendant was her ticket out of Kansas City, Missouri. Flying internationally, she was exposed to cuisines from all around the globe.

On her first trip to Paris, she was blown away by the food. In contrast to the United States, where the soul food she grew up with was often demeaned, the French celebrated humble food that had roots in the countryside.

In addition to flying around the globe, Deborah followed her husband, whose pro basketball career took him to France, Spain, Italy, Israel, the Philippines, Argentina, and Switzerland. Everywhere she visited, her palate was honed on new flavors and ingredients.

When her labor union went on strike in 1993, Deborah took her passion for cooking more seriously and enrolled in the culinary school at the Art Institute of Atlanta. For a few years, she straddled two worlds, operating a catering company while continuing her airline job.

In 1998, Deborah opened Edible Arts, a 28-seat restaurant in East Atlanta Village. She painted thrift store chairs and decoupaged tables for an artistic decor. Her menu was equally creative, with playful versions of classic soul food dishes. Her signature Southern Marinated Fried Chicken and Three-Cheese Macaroni were accompanied by a sweet potato apple chutney (a healthier alternative to candied yams) and a collard green roll (think of stuffed grape leaves, and then replace both the grape leaf and the stuffing with collards).

After a move to Underground Atlanta did not pan out, Deborah, who was going through a divorce, put the restaurant on the back burner so she could focus on raising her daughter, Kursten, and catering.

Left: Lamb T-bone with carrot puree and farm fresh vegetables. Center: Chef Deborah VanTrece mixes classic Southern dishes with influences from around the globe. *Top right:* Chicken-Fried Duck with sawmill andouille gravy and mixed spring vegetables. *Above right:* Bucatini with lobster, prawns, scallops, seafood brodo, and fried basil. All photos by Henri Hollis.

With Kursten grown, Deborah opened Twisted Soul in Decatur in 2014. In 2016, she relocated to her current location in the Westside.

Inspired by her travels abroad, Deborah reinvents dishes she grew up with. Her Hoisin Oxtails give an Asian twist to a humble Southern favorite. The dish was inspired by an article she read about oxtails in Asian cuisine and a hoisin lamb dish she served in first-class during her flight attendant days.

Today, Twisted Soul is a family affair. Deborah co-owns the restaurant with her wife, Lorraine Lane, and her daughter, now Kursten Berry, serves as beverage director. Her creative cocktails match her mother's unique menu. Where else will you find a martini with pot liquor (the broth leftover from cooking collards)?

1133 Huff Rd. NW #D
(404) 350-5500
twistedsoulcookhouseandpours.com

The cocktail menu is as unique as the dinner menu! Don't miss the Southern Hospitality (gin, pot liquor, pressed apple, and Tabasco pepper) or the Liquid Soul (moonshine mixed with Kursten's own "Kool-Aid," made from hibiscus, cherries, and lemongrass).

FLYING BISCUIT

Teamwork makes the creamy dreamy grits work

As a waitress at Indigo Coastal Grille in Atlanta, Delia Champion would sit with the other servers at the start of their shift, drinking coffee and polishing silverware. As they worked, they daydreamed. "When I own a restaurant . . ." was a familiar start to a sentence as they imagined how they would run things differently if they were in charge.

"When I own a restaurant, we'll serve breakfast all day," imagined Delia. Working in "the industry," she usually worked late and then went out until three or four in the morning, so sleeping until the afternoon was the norm. By the time she'd wake up, most restaurants were done serving breakfast.

She spoke so often of her breakfast-all-day dream that a friend came back from a vacation with a name in tow: "The Flying Biscuit." Now Delia's daydreams began, "At the Flying Biscuit. . . ."

But how does a waitress start a restaurant? She teams up with friends. She, Cynthia Moore, and Missy Speert pooled their resources, and Delia's good friend Emily Sailers (of the Indigo Girls) gave her a loan. But the teamwork didn't end there; employees (and friends) contributed recipes. Delia also credits her accountant, Richard Rathsack, for his sage counsel.

"No one person can do it alone," says Delia.

Cynthia, Missy, and Delia opened the original Flying Biscuit in Candler Park in 1993, and it's been a neighborhood staple ever since.

While you'll find breakfast classics such as omelettes, benedicts, and pancakes, you'll also find less-traditional dishes, such as Egg-Ceptional Eggs (two eggs on black bean cakes with tomatillo salsa, feta cheese, and sour cream) and the Egg-Straordinary Breakfast (two eggs, creamy dreamy grits, and oven-roasted moon-dusted potatoes). And, yes, there are biscuits at the Flying Biscuit. They're

Left: The High Flyer—two eggs served with, chicken sausage, moon-dusted potatoes, pancake, and, of course, a flying biscuit. *Right:* The Southern Benedict at the Flying Biscuit, a split biscuit topped with pimento cheese, two over medium eggs, bacon, hollandaise, and basil, served with creamy dreamy grits.

the perfect vehicle for Chef April Moon's cranberry apple butter.

Over the years, Delia bought out her partners. In 2006, she sold the company to an Atlanta-based franchise company. Today, the original two Flying Biscuits have been joined by more than 20 franchises across Georgia, Alabama, both Carolinas, Florida, and Texas. Delia now focuses attention on her newest venture, Delia's Chicken Sausage (see page 164).

While you'll find their signature biscuits at any of the stores, it's worth making a pilgrimage to the original location in Candler Park, with its funky murals and oil cloth–covered tables. Good luck trying to decide between the oven-roasted moon-dusted potatoes and the creamy dreamy grits!

Candler Park (The Original):
1655 McLendon Ave.
404-687-888
flyingbiscuit.com

Don't have time to sit down for a full breakfast? At the Candler Park location, there's a separate entrance for to-go orders where you can pick up a single biscuit or a dozen.

CHAI PANI & BOTIWALLA

Changing American perception of Indian cuisine

It took Meherwan Irani three careers and a recession to start cooking professionally, but five James Beard nominations later, he's revolutionizing Indian cuisine in the states.

At age 4, Meherwan and his family moved from London to live with his grandmother in Ahmednagar, India, a small town popular with western pilgrims. Their home was a bed and breakfast where his mother cooked approachable Indian meals and punched-up American dishes for guests.

When Meherwan moved to South Carolina for business school, he was appalled by the heavy, greasy, over-spiced food served at Indian buffet restaurants. He began cooking for himself, frequently calling mom for advice and recipes.

Following careers in importing jewelry and selling luxury cars in San Francisco, Meherwan and his wife, Molly, moved to Asheville, where he sold real estate until the 2009 recession devastated the industry. Instead of finding another "safe" job, Molly encouraged her husband to follow his passion. After complaining for years about the poor quality of Indian restaurants, perhaps he could change how Americans view Indian food. By the next morning, he had crafted a menu, drawn a floor plan, and decided on a name for his restaurant—Chai Pani.

Literally translated as "tea and water," *chai pani* is slang for going out for a cup of tea or a snack. Instead of focusing on cuisine from a

Stop by Chai Pani on a weekend night for a visit to the pani puri cart for crisp fried dough balls (*puri*) dunked in a spicy, tangy water and stuffed with a mashed potato mixture made to order. On weekdays from 3 to 5 p.m, Botiwalla serves Irani Cafe High Tea–house-brewed masala chai, Parle-G cookies, *tea rusk* (milk toast), and *maska pav* (toasted rolls with butter and jam).

Left: Meherwan Irani is on a mission to change how Americans think about Indian cuisine. Photo by Tim Robison. *Center:* Botiwalla in Ponce City Market is a fast-casual spot specializing in grilled meats. Photo by Lauren Van Epps. *Right:* The Kale Pakoras are an addictive, savory snack with a little kick. Photo by Molly Milroy.

specific region, Meherwan was drawn to cooking Indian street food. He interviewed several Indian chefs who knew how to make chicken *tikka masala* or *saag paneer* but were clueless about street food. Instead, he hired young chefs and flew in his mother to lead a three-month boot camp in Indian home-cooking. To this day, he annually sends a team of employees on a street food adventure in India.

His Asheville location was so popular that he opened a larger version in Decatur, Georgia.

Meherwan recommends the Vada Pav, a spicy fried potato dumpling sandwich. The crispy julienned okra fries are his mother's recipe (the only way she could get her kids to touch okra). Curly kale leaves provide the perfect canvas for the curried chickpea batter of Kale Pakoras.

With the opening of Ponce City Market, Meherwan debuted Botiwalla, inspired by grilled meats cooked streetside on *sigiris* (charcoal grills) and found in *Irani cafes* (kebab houses in India run by Irani immigrants).

Don't expect simple sandwiches. The Chicken Tikka, Paneer, and Lamb Boti Kebab Rolls are served in a hot buttered naan, overflowing with desi slaw, onions, cilantro, chutney, and flavor.

Chai Pani
406 W Ponce de Leon Ave., Decatur
404-378-4030
chaipanidecatur.com

Botiwalla
Ponce City Market,
675 Ponce De Leon Ave. NE
470-225-8963
botiwalla.com

THE VORTEX

Great burgers, but no idiots

In 1991, graphic designer Michael Benoit had grown tired of living in LA, and he was ready to move to a "small town." During a two-week road trip across the southeast, he fell in love with Atlanta nightlife. In those days, last call was 4 a.m., and some joints never closed. Mike convinced his brother Hank to join him, and their sister Susanne soon followed.

The siblings decided to open a bar. According to Michael, their logic was simple, "We like going to bars, why don't we open one and then we'll be in a bar every day?" Despite having little restaurant experience, the siblings assumed the lease of Stang's Bar & Grill, located in the ground floor of a Marriott Residence Inn.

With no budget for decor, they threw a "Bring Us Your Crap Party," inviting friends to donate art, taxidermied animals, or other unwanted items. Michael describes the resulting decor as something resembling "your crazy aunt's attic."

On a given night, you might rub elbows with bikers, artists, or bankers. For the most part, everyone gets along, but early on Michael had to kick out one guy who always gave the staff grief. Soon after, he posted their first house rule: "The Vortex Is an Official Idiot-Free Zone."

In a place that celebrates debauchery with its motto "it's good to be bad," and through its decor of motorcycles, booze, and pin-ups, it's a little surprising to find two pages of the menu dedicated to "the rules." Written in an irreverent tone, the rules are fun to read, but that doesn't mean you shouldn't take them seriously.

The Vortex's signature burgers won't be found anywhere else. Satisfy your adventure urge by ordering a Fat Elvis (smothered with peanut butter, bacon, and plantains) or a Hell's Fury (pepper jack cheese, Atomic Death Sauce, habanero relish, and a roasted jalapeño).

Top left: The Classic Bypass is topped with a fried egg, three slices of American cheese, four slices of bacon, lettuce, tomato, onion, and pickles. *Above left:* Siblings Hank, Susanne, and Michael Benoit joined forces to open The Vortex. *Right:* The skull entrance to the Little 5 Points Vortex is iconic.

If your life insurance is paid up, you may want to order from the Coronary Bypass menu, where the buns are bacon-grilled cheese sandwiches. The quadruple weighs in with an estimated 9,606 calories.

In the mid '90s, the owners closed the original location and opened two new ones. Driving through Little Five Points, it's impossible to miss the huge skull that frames the front door of The Vortex. The midtown location includes the popular comedy club, the Laughing Skull Lounge.

Midtown:
878 Peachtree St. NE
404-875-1667

Little Five Points:
438 Moreland Ave.
404-688-1828

thevortexatl.com

Many retired dishes are available on the secret menu, which is hidden on their website. Like any hidden treasure, you have to think like a pirate.

BUFORD HIGHWAY

Six miles of global fare

There may be 71 streets named Peachtree in Atlanta, but there's only one road that allows you to eat your way across the world—Buford Highway.

At first glance, Buford Highway looks like any other stretch of suburban sprawl, with fast-food restaurants, gas stations, and strip malls. But a closer look reveals signs for Mexican *carnicerias* (meat market), Salvadoran *pupuserias* (a place that sells *pupusas*: thick, corn griddle cake filled with meats, cheese, or beans), and Chinese dim sum.

In other major cities, neighborhoods are often divided into ethnic enclaves. But on Buford Highway, global ethnicities are intertwined. For example, Guatemalan bakery Xela Pan Cafe, Korean Sokongdong Tofu House, and Mexican taqueria El Rey Del Taco share the same parking lot.

Often called the "international coordinator," this section of State Route 13, which straddles Gwinnett, Fulton, and DeKalb counties, is lined with more than 1,000 immigrant-owned businesses, at least 100 of them restaurants. The majority are owned by immigrants from Korea, Mexico, China, and Vietnam, but you'll also find Indian, Bangladeshi, Indonesian, Central American, Somali, and Ethiopian owners as well.

The highway was built in the 1930s as part of the Works Progress Administration (WPA) project to connect Atlanta to the countryside near the Buford Dam. Suburban development began in the 1960s as affordable apartment buildings popped up, mainly catering to white, blue-collar families.

Havana Sandwich Shop (page 156) is credited as the first immigrant-owned restaurant on Buford Highway, opening its doors in 1979. During subsequent decades, first-generation families from

Top left: Havana Sandwich Shop was the first international restaurant to open on Buford Highway back in 1979. *Above left:* James Beard–nominated Chef Atsushi Hayakawa can be found behind the sushi bar every night at Sushi Hayakawa on Buford Highway. *Right:* Sweet Hut (pictured), White Windmill Bakery, and Mozart Bakery serve a variety of Asian baked goods.

Asia and Latin America saw that Buford Highway could be their ticket to the American Dream, offering reasonable rent, access to public transportation, and proximity to jobs.

Today, Buford Highway and the neighboring communities of Doraville and Chamblee contain some of the most diverse populations in the Southeast.

It's next to impossible to have a bad meal on Buford Highway. Don't let a nondescript exterior or lackluster decor fool you. If the parking lot is full and most of the tables are occupied, chances are the food is delicious and affordable.

Pull into any of the strip malls along Buford Highway for a variety of culinary delights. For example, Asian Square houses Good Harvest (modern Chinese and hot pot), Ding Tea (Taiwanese teahouse), Quoc Huong (banh mi Sandwiches), King Skewer (meat skewers), Ming's BBQ (Cantonese), and La Mei Zi (Taiwanese and Sichuan dishes). For dessert, stop by Roll It Up for rolled ice cream, Sweet Spot for an ice cream bowl or a Fleecy, a Hong-Kong-style milkshake.

The only difficult thing about dining on Buford Highway is knowing where to begin. Here's my unofficial, incomplete guide to dining on Buford Highway (and a few places just off the main drag).

Barkot (Ethiopian)
2857 Buford Hwy. NE

Bismillah Cafe (Indian)
4022 Buford Hwy. NE

BoBo Garden (Cantonese)
5181 Buford Hwy. NE

Canton House (Dim sum)
4825 Buford Hwy. NE

Crawfish Shack
(Cajun-Vietnamese seafood)
4337 Buford Hwy. NE

El Rey del Taco (Atlanta's first taqueria)
5288 Buford Hwy. NE

Co'M Vietnamese Grill (Vietnamese)
4005 Buford Hwy. NE

Deshi Street (Bangladeshi)
4337 Buford Hwy. NE

Food Terminal (Malaysian)
5000 Buford Hwy. NE

Good Harvest (Chinese hot pot)
5150 Buford Hwy. NE

Good Luck Gourmet
(Xi'an-style Chinese)
5750 Buford Hwy. NE

Gu's Kitchen (Szechuan)
4897 Buford Hwy. NE

Halal Guys (Middle Eastern)
4929 Buford Hwy. NE

Havana Sandwich Shop (Cuban)
2905 Buford Hwy. NE

Kang Nam (Japanese)
5715 Buford Hwy. NE

La Mei Zi (Chinese-Taiwanese)
5150 Buford Hwy. NE

LanZhoa
(hand-pulled Chinese noodles)
5231 Buford Hwy. NE

Little Lagos (Nigerian)
3979 Buford Hwy. NE

Mamak (Malaysian)
5150 Buford Hwy. NE

Marisqueria El Veneno
(Mexican seafood)
5082 Buford Hwy. NE

Masterpiece (Sichuan Chinese)
3940 Buford Hwy. NE

Nam Phuong (Vietnamese)
4051 Buford Hwy. NE

Left: El Rey Del Taco was one of the first taquerias on Buford Highway. *Right:* Food Terminal is the newest Malaysian restaurant on Buford Highway.

Northern China Eatery (Dumplings)
5141 Buford Hwy. NE

Penang (Malaysian)
4897 Buford Hwy. NE

Plaza Fiesta (Latin shopping mall)
4166 Buford Hwy. NE

Pho Dai Loi #2 (Vietnamese)
4186 Buford Hwy. NE

Purnima (Bangladeshi)
4646 Buford Hwy. NE

Quoc Huong (banh mi sandwiches)
5150 Buford Hwy. NE

Rican Latino (Salvadorian)
5055 Buford Hwy. NE

Sabores del Plata
(Argentinian-Uruguayan)
6200 Buford Hwy. NE

Sinaloense Pollos Asados
(Mexican)
5303 Buford Hwy. NE

Sokongdong Tofu House (Korean)
5280 Buford Hwy. NE

Sushi Hayakawa
(sushi omakase)
5979 Buford Hwy. NE

Sweet Hut Bakery and Cafe
(Asian-inspired bakery)
5150 Buford Hwy. NE

Tasty 21 (Chinese Hot Pot)
5979 Buford Hwy. NE

Xela Pan Cafe
(Guatemalan bakery)
5268 Buford Hwy. NE

Yet Tuh (Korean)
3042 Oakcliff Rd.

Playful prix fixe

After attending culinary school, Jarrett Stieber cut his teeth in some of the best kitchens in Atlanta: Pura Vida, Restaurant Eugene, Holeman & Finch, Abattoir, and Empire State South.

Burned out on the long hours, low pay, and emotionally draining environment, Jarrett was considering quitting the industry when friend Dale Donchey, who had lost his lease for Steady Hand Pour House in Emory Village, invited him to provide the food menu for his new breakfast/lunch pop-up at Iberian Pig.

Over six years, Jarrett built a following for his Eat Me Speak Me pop-up, which took up long-term residencies at Candler Park Market, General Muir, Gato, and SOS Tiki Bar. The small menu changed weekly, based on what local farmers had available.

In 2019, he retired the Eat Me Speak Me pop-up concept to focus on opening his own restaurant. Named for Fernando, Jarrett's Pyrenees mountain dog that resembles a bear, Little Bear is a 30-seat neighborhood restaurant located in the gentrifying Summerhill. Each dish showcased Jarrett's creativity and flare.

In early 2020, after six years of preparation, Jarrett opened Little Bear—just weeks before the pandemic hit.

Jarrett and his team quickly changed formats. They ditched the a la carte menu and tasting-menu options, and offered Just F**k Me Up, Fam . . . But To Go, a prix fixe dinner for two.

The menu changed from week to week, often including playful takes on a different region of the world. During Peruvian Chifa Week, the Mazamorra Morada y Chocolate, a blue hominy pudding, was adorned with Peruvian bittersweet chocolate, peaches, assorted crispy things, soft herbs, and pretentious flowers. And the menu explained that the Pollo Tipakay con Arroz Chaufa had marinated chanterelles "cus we FAN-CY."

Left: Jarrett Stieber finally opened his first restaurant in February 2020, less than a month before the city shut down for quarantine. Photo by Kate Blohm. *Center:* Mazamorra Morada—a sweet Peruvian purple corn pudding, topped with fresh peaches, edible flowers, and puffed rice. *Right:* Jarrett's take on the Peruivan-Chineses Pollo Tipakay con Arroz Chaufa (sweet and sour chicken with fried rice).

Turns out that Jarrett loved the new format. Creating one set menu each week allowed him to be creative while keeping costs low. The new format worked so well that he has decided that after the pandemic, Little Bear will reopen as tasting-menu-only.

Unlike other tasting menus that can easily set you back $100 a person or more, Little Bear will offer four courses (two vegetables, one protein, and a dessert) at a modest price.

The new menu still reflects his vision for a tiny, hole-in-the-wall, neighborhood restaurant with casual atmosphere, where the food is better than it should be for the price point—a more approachable and affordable take on fine dining.

71 Georgia Ave. SE, Suite A
404-500-5396
littlebearatl.com

No, you won't know what they'll be serving, but you can visit the Little Bear website to see the most recent menu. They're happy to accommodate dietary restrictions. There's always a vegetarian alternative for the protein, but it's a good idea to call a day ahead with any other allergies or restrictions.

TALAT MARKET

Creating Georgian Thai cuisine

"When people asked me what's a good Thai place, I never had a good answer," says Parnass Savang. "They all have cookie-cutter menus. It's not what they eat at home. They just cook it because it's what customers expect."

Growing up in his parents' Thai restaurant, Danthai, in Lawrenceville, Georgia, meant one thing: chores, and lots of them. It wasn't until he binge-watched the British version of *Kitchen Nightmares* that Parnass took an interest in the restaurant industry. Watching Gordon Ramsay rescue struggling restaurants, he imagined what he could do for his parents' restaurant.

Wanting to learn from the best, Parnass attended the Culinary Institute of America and spent almost a decade cooking in some of the most celebrated kitchens in Atlanta.

While working together at Kimball House, Parnass and Rod Lassiter cooked up the idea for Talat Market, where Parnass would implement lessons he learned in culinary school and cooking at Empire State South, Staplehouse, and Kimball House, and apply them to Thai cuisine.

Though they imagined a small brick-and-mortar restaurant, they decided to follow the path laid by fellow Empire State South alum Jarrett Steiber (see page 126), who created a following with his weekly Eat Me Speak Me pop-up.

For a year and a half, Talat Market was the pop-up-in-residence at Gato in Candler Park. With only 30 seats, throngs of hungry guests

> For a complete Thai dinner, come with friends and order one dish from each category on the menu. Don't miss the fruit salad (an homage to Parnass's maternal grandparents, who sold pineapples in a fruit market) and Red Curry (a favorite dish from his dad's side of the family).

Left: Talat Market's doors opened during the pandemic. They pivoted to take-out only, leaving the dining room vacant for months. *Top center:* Rod Lassiter and Parnass Savang created the idea for Talat Market while working together at Kimball House. *Above center:* The Red Curry is based on the family favorite from Parnass's dad's side of the family. *Right:* A traditional Thai family meal would include a variety of dishes, including salad, stir-fry, soup, rice, vegetables, and something fried or grilled.

waited eagerly outside. After their first year, Parnass was nominated as a James Beard Foundation Rising Star Chef Semifinalist, and their pop-up was named one of the 50 best restaurants in America by *Bon Appetit.*

In 2018, Parnass and Rod retired the weekly pop-ups to focus on opening the restaurant. For the next two years, they refined their menu and built out the space while hosting sold out pop-ups and restaurant takeovers across the city.

Just as they were finally ready to open, the pandemic hit. But that didn't stop the Talat team. Each week, they offered a prix fixe dinner for two and cocktail kits to-go.

But the plan was always to return to the original concept—a menu based on a typical Thai family meal featuring local ingredients. Guests select from two options in each category: salad, relish with vegetables, curry, stir-fry, soup, rice, and something fried or grilled.

The result: Thai food that goes against the grain, while honoring traditional Thai flavors and ingredients.

112 Ormond St. SE
404-257-6255
talatmarketatl.com

EL SUPER PAN &
EL BURRO POLLO

Pushing Latin American cuisine forward

For a college assignment to interview a businessperson, Hector Santiago chose Chef Giovanna Huyke, who, like Hector, was from San Juan, Puerto Rico. She offered Hector a job on the spot—as a dishwasher.

Chef Huyke took maternity leave six months later, but not before instilling in her young protégé a passion for fresh ingredients and a willingness to break rules to advance Puerto Rican cuisine. His next mentor, a New Orleans–trained chef, tutored him in the use of blackened rubs, a skill he employs today in his own *adobo* (spice mixture).

Despite two years at the Culinary Institute of America, Hector, whom many will remember from Season 6 of *Top Chef*, says his real education came from sampling Latin American eateries in New York City and from cooking alongside classmates from other countries.

After three years up north, Hector and his partner moved to Atlanta prior to the 1996 Olympics. Hector was hired as chef at Roswell's Public House.

A few years later, Hector opened Pura Vida, a pan-Latin concept featuring an extensive tapas menu. His dishes were inspired by frequent trips to both Latin America and the Buford Highway Farmers Market.

Hector has definitely pushed Latin cuisine forward. His French Mofongo, for example, is his interpretation of a Puerto Rican standard: garlicky mashed plantains paired with sweet peas and truffles.

To encourage guests to focus on tapas, Hector removed burritos and sandwiches from the menu and began offering them at Super Pan, a lunch spot he opened downstairs, which was inspired by Puerto Rican bakeries.

Left: The Super Cubano is the most popular sandwich on the Super Pan menu. *Center left:* Chef Hector Santiago poses with his famous El Burro Pollo. *Center right:* Sofrito Chicken Mofongo (garlic mashed plantains served with sofrito chicken and a chicken broth) at Super Pan. *Right:* Shrimp al Ajillo Rice & Bean Bowl (brown rice, pink beans, roasted carrots, and shrimp sautéed with garlic and onion) and the Farm Cubano (veggie Cuban) at Super Pan.

On Saturdays, Hector sold spicy chicken burritos in the parking lot. Chicken, slow-cooked with copious amounts of chiles, was topped with fresh slaw to cut the heat, wrapped in a slightly charred tortilla, and served in pages of *Creative Loafing*. His El Burro Pollos soon gained cult status.

Skyrocketing rents moved Hector to close Pura Vida and Super Pan in 2012. After a stint at Anne Quatrano's Abattoir, he reopened Super Pan in the Ponce City Market Food Hall. While the Cuban sandwich is the most popular item; for a real Puerto Rican treat, try the Mofongo Bowl with Shrimp.

In addition to sandwiches and bowls available at PCM, Hector's more spacious Battery Park location offers full brunch, lunch, dinner, and cocktail menus.

For years, his burritos were available only at pop-ups, but in 2020, Hector opened his first El Burro Pollo stand at the Collective Food Hall at Coda. The famous chicken burritos are joined by an assortment of ceviches, pozoles, and other burritos.

Ponce City Market	The Battery Atlanta	El Burro Pollo
675 Ponce de Leon Ave. NE	455 Legends Pl.	756 W. Peachtree St. NW
404-600-2465	404-521-6500	470-312-4406
elsuperpan.com		elburropollo.com

Vegetarians will want to order the Smoked Tofu Cubano at Super Pan or the Smoked Tofu Burrito at El Burro Pollo.

131

BATAVIA

Atlanta's first Indonesian restaurant

How did an immigrant from China come to own Atlanta's first Indonesian restaurant and grocery store?

Chinese-born Iris Li met Indonesian-native Lisa Kou when they were both working for a wholesale company in Atlanta. Although Atlanta had an Indonesian population of at least 7,000 at the time, there were no Indonesian restaurants catering to the community, and Indonesian products were hard to find.

So Lisa and Iris decided to go into business together and open Batavia, named for the former capital of the Dutch East Indies (now known as Jakarta). The restaurant/grocery was a welcome addition, not only to Atlanta's Indonesian community, but also to the city's foodies.

When visa complications forced Lisa to return to Indonesia in 2009, Iris took full ownership of the restaurant, hiring Indonesian chefs, including Chef Nanang, who has been at Batavia for more than 10 years.

Indonesian cuisine is varied, in no small part because the country contains more than 6,000 inhabited islands, each with its own culinary tradition. Soups, noodles, and rice dishes, characterized by complex sweet and spicy flavors, are found throughout the country.

Start your meal with *gado-gado*, a traditional salad of cucumbers, boiled eggs, tofu, and tempe served with a peanut sauce and garlic crackers. More than 15 spices are used to create *rendang*, a spicy beef

Flavors vary greatly from island to island in Indonesia. Some like it spicier, others more sour. Iris encourages you to request your dish the way you like it. To accompany your meal, pick out an Indonesian tea or soursop juice from the cooler on the far wall. Homemade desserts, such as *martabak*, a stuffed pancake filled with chocolate, peanuts, or cheese, are availble on Saturdays and Sundays.

Left: Gule Kambing, a savory, slightly spicy, lamb stew in coconut milk. *Center:* Not sure what to order? Check out the hot bar, where you can feast with your eyes before deciding what to have. *Top right:* The grocery offers a huge selection of Indonesian snacks and ingredients, such as *kerupuk* (deep-fried crackers) in a variety of shapes and flavors. *Above right:* Nasi *Bakar Bandung*, salt fish and chili wrapped in rice and a banana leaf, served with homemade tempe, fried tofu, and a chicken drumstick. All photos by Adrienne Bruce.

stew. *Bakso malang* is a noodle soup that combines two traditional dishes: *bakso* (meatballs) and *bakwan malang* (a fried wonton soup from the city of Malang). Lamb fans will love the *gulai kambing* (a rich lamb curry from Sumatra) and lamb *satay* (skewered, grilled lamb).

Following a common trend in Indonesia, almost half of the restaurant's space serves as a grocery store. It's one of the few places Indonesian home-cooks can pick up familiar spice blends. There's an extensive selection of *kerupuk*, deep-fried crackers in an assortment of shapes and flavors. These savory snacks can be purchased ready to eat or for frying and are usually eaten along with stews.

Although most of the products are imported, the *tempe* (tempeh) is made in-house. This traditional Indonesian soy product is especially popular on the island of Java, where it's one of the main sources of protein. The culturing and fermentation process binds soybeans into a firm, textured cake, which is commonly used as a meat alternative. Try the *tempe* as an appetizer or entrée, and take a block home with you.

3640 Shallowford Rd., Doraville
404 254-0646
bataviadoravilletogo.com

TAQUERIA DEL SOL

South by southwest

Growing up in Monterey, Mexico, Eddie Hernandez learned to cook from his grandmother, but he didn't imagine a career in the kitchen. He wanted to be on stage.

After moving to Waco, Texas, as a teenager, Eddie played drums for Fascinación, a Latin rock band. Known for getting audiences dancing, Fascinación was a popular opening act for touring bands in Mexico and the US. When he wasn't performing, Eddie cooked for his bandmates.

By 1987, Eddie had had enough of the late nights, heavy drinking, and other aspects of life on the road, so he moved to Atlanta.

His first job was at El Azteca, a Mexican restaurant in Clayton County. He quickly befriended owner Mike Klank. The two later opened Azteca Grill, where Eddie created a menu that more closely resembled dishes he grew up with in Mexico.

In 1991, they opened Sundown Cafe, a more upscale restaurant that fused Southern dishes with Southwestern flavors: shrimp cakes with chipotle cream sauce or a blue corn–crusted tilapia with a poblano tartar sauce.

When a regular brought Eddie fresh turnip greens from his garden, he had no idea what to do with them. Mike took him to Mary Macs (see page 64), where they definitely know how to cook turnip greens. Inspired, Eddie created his own version using Mexican spices, chicken stock, and dried peppers.

To supplement their dinner business, they offered Southern-influenced tacos at lunch. Guests ordered and paid at the counter before finding a table. Today we're accustomed to the fast-casual routine, but in 1992, it was new to customers. For Eddie and Mike, it was a good way to turn tables quickly and keep prices low.

When developers at Westside Provisions approached Eddie and Mike about opening a concept restaurant, they created Taqueria del

Left: Shrimp corn chowder with fried chicken and brisket tacos. *Center:* Taqueria del Sol co-owners Eddie Hernandez and Mike Klank. *Right:* Taqueria del Sol combines Mexican dishes with southern ingredients.

Sol, fully embracing Southern/Southwestern fast casual. In 2005, they closed Sundown Cafe to open their third Taqueria del Sol.

South meets Southwest in the soft tacos: the Memphis (chopped smoked pork with spicy jalapeño coleslaw and tequila BBQ sauce), Brisket (with pico de gallo), and Fried Chicken (with a jalapeño mayo).

The enchiladas are designed so guests can mix and match fillings and sauces. The shrimp corn chowder is prepared using techniques Eddie learned from an exchange with a French restaurant.

In addition to three weekly specials (one new creation and two favorites from the past), one off-the-menu item is always available— The George (a bowl of charros beans, turnip greens, and rice).

Westside:
1200-B Howell Mill Rd.
404-352-5811

359 W. Ponce de Leon Ave.,
Decatur
404-377-7668

Cheshire Bridge:
2165 Cheshire Bridge Rd.
404-321-1118

5001 Peachtree Blvd., Suite 910,
Chamblee
470-321-3232

taqueriadelsol.com

Do not sit down. Resist the temptation to have someone in your party hold a table while you wait in line. Trust that the system works. You will find a table after your order, and magically a server will find you and bring you your food.

PAOLO'S GELATO ITALIANO

The scoop behind Atlanta's first gelateria

Paolo Dalla Zorza, a native of Italy, has reinvented himself numerous times. When he was 13, he claims, he was the youngest professional magician in Italy.

Although Paolo was groomed to take over the family pharmacy, he had other plans. A fierce animal lover, Paolo trained as a veterinarian, which led to a position as a meatpacking inspector. Always eager to try something new, Paolo moved to the US to earn his pilot's license.

One thing he soon noticed about his new country was the absence of gelato—Italy's gift to the world of ice cream. Presto chango! Paolo decided to introduce his new homeland to gelato. One catch: he knew nothing about making it. That led to trips to Italy, Spain, Germany, and Japan to learn different techniques.

During a layover in Atlanta, Paolo decided to explore Virginia Highlands, which had been suggested by a friend. While touring the neighborhood, he spotted a vacant storefront displaying a sign for Italian ices. The landlord was reluctant to take on another tenant selling frozen desserts, but Paolo used some of his magical charm to seal the deal. Twenty years later, Paolo's Gelato Italiano is an Atlanta culinary landmark.

Way back then, few Atlantans were familiar with gelato, so Paolo gave out free samples—lots of free samples. During his first year, Paolo estimates he used about 55,000 sample spoons.

Flavors change daily, so follow Paolo's on Instagram to see what's on the menu. Most of the flavors are gluten-free, and the fruit flavors are dairy-free. Even dogs can get into the fun; treat yours to Paolo's soy-based, sugar-free pet gelato.

Left: Paolo Dalla Zorza is eager to share his love of Italian desserts. *Middle:* The creamy gelatos are made in-house. *Right:* A cup of Paolo's gelato is always more than just a cup of gelato.

Over time, his customers came to love such flavors as *stracciatella* (vanilla with flakes of chocolate), *zuppa Inglese* (custard base with bits of cake and sherry), *castagna* (chestnuts), *zabaione* (egg yolks with sweet marsala wine), and *vino rosso* (Italian red wine).

One flavor you won't find at Paolo's? Vanilla. "When people would order vanilla, I send them to Ben & Jerry's!" Paolo exclaims.

Originally, he imported gelato cups and spoons, but he saw an opportunity to turn fellow gelato purveyors from competitors to customers. He started a side business, manufacturing and distributing gelato supplies.

Paolo sold Gelato Supply to devote more time to his two gelato stores (one in Charleston, South Carolina, as well as his original store in Virginia Highlands). Ever the self-reinventor, he recently started a line of Italian food products, including pasta, sauces, vinegars, antipasto, and olive oil, which are available online or at his stores.

1025 Virginia Ave NE
404-607-0055
paolosgelato.com

57TH FIGHTER GROUP RESTAURANT

A side of history and an air show for dessert

At the end of a kudzu-lined drive, past abandoned military jeeps and a guard post, a bombed-out French farmhouse awaits. Suddenly, you're in World War II Europe. The only things missing are planes flying overhead. . . . Wait, the 57th Fighter Group Restaurant has those, too.

David Compton Tallichet Jr., volunteered as a bomber pilot when the US entered World War II. Following the war, he earned the moniker "father of themed restaurants" when he joined SeaWorld founder George Millay to start the Specialty Restaurant Corporation. In 1958, the Polynesian-themed Reef Restaurant in Long Beach, California, became their first of more than 100 theme restaurants.

The 57th Fighter Group, at the DeKalb Peachtree Airport (PDK), opened in 1981, replete with stucco walls, exposed beams, and huge fireplaces. To imbue the faux farmhouse with a battle-damaged feel, they distressed the exterior and lined the entrance walls with sandbags.

Inside, walls are plastered with WWII memorabilia—black and white photos, a silk map highlighting escape routes for POWs, and a captured Nazi flag. In the lounge, veterans are invited to sign wooden planks honoring American Heroes.

The restaurant closed in 2000. Years later, when it was slated to be torn down for another hanger, Pat Epps, an Air Force Veteran and owner of Epps Aviation, purchased the building. He had dual motives: to perpetuate the homage to WWII veterans and also to keep competitors from acquiring the property. The 57th Fighter Group Restaurant reopened in 2009 and has been high-flying ever since.

Left: Abandoned military jeeps are the first sign that you're not in Atlanta anymore. *Center:* The rich and creamy Beer Cheese Soup is a house specialty. *Top right:* Sit out on the patio or by the windows for a view of the DeKalb Peachtree Airport runway. *Above right:* The burgers are made with trimmings from the hand-cut steaks.

Pat enhanced the decor by writing and framing short bios of friends who served, and he added the Bunker Room to showcase photos and memorabilia from the Vietnam War.

On one side of the building, huge windows overlook the runways, offering the best floor show in town. With an average of 228,000 takeoffs and landings a year, PDK is the second-busiest airport in Georgia. The planes are small, but sitting so close is big fun.

Even without the views and history, the food would be worth the visit. The Southern-inspired American menu features the 57th Sandwich (shaved steak, caramelized onion, and beer cheese sauce), catfish and hushpuppies, a reuben, and a cajun shrimp boil. Rich and creamy, their signature Beer Cheese Soup, topped with crispy bacon, is sinfully addictive. The steaks are hand-cut each day, and the trimmings are ground to make some of the most delicious burgers in the city.

3829 Clairmont Rd.
770-234-0057
the57threstaurant.com

Request to be seated by the windows or on the patio for a front row seat of the runway. If you're seated in the booths, ask for a pair of headsets so you can listen to the control tower at the airport. Be sure to visit the restroom to hear Winston Churchill deliver excerpts of some of his most famous speeches.

VIRGIL'S GULLAH KITCHEN & BAR

A taste of the Lowcountry

Husbands Gregory (Gee) and Juan Smalls did not set out to open Atlanta's only Gullah/Geechee Restaurant.

The couple ran a successful event production business and a nonprofit, The Gentlemen's Foundation, which hosts an annual ball to celebrate LGBTQ African Americans who are making a difference in the community.

They saw a need for a space for Atlanta's Black LGBTQ community, owned by people in the community. With their event-planning experience, the Smalls drafted a business plan to open a bar/lounge where their community would feel safe and welcome.

When they started creating a menu, it was a no-brainer: Gee loved to cook and wanted to share the Gullah Geechee dishes he grew up with in Charleston, South Carolina. Before long, their vision of a lounge evolved into a full-scale Gullah Geechee restaurant that would cater to everyone.

The Gullah Geechee people were originally brought in slave ships from West Africa to the coastal islands of South Carolina, Georgia, and Florida to grow rice, indigo, and cotton. Because their communities were separated from the mainland and the plantation economy collapsed after the Civil War, their distinctive culture was preserved into recent times.

> Be sure to check out the table decorations. The "roses" are handcrafted by Gullah Geechee people from Charleston, South Carolina, using leaves of the Sabal Palm (or Palmetto tree), the state tree of South Carolina.

Left: Afta Church Plate is the classic soul food dish often served after church on Sundays. *Center:* Owners and husbands, Gee and Juan take a picture on Grand Opening day in front of Virgil's. *Top right:* Slammin Sammen—blackened Atlantic salmon topped with a crab cream sauce, fried oysters, and shrimp, with white rice and Geechee fried corn.

"Soul food was created in Gullah Geechee culture," says Gee, who learned to cook from his family. His father, the restaurant's namesake, taught him to make Shrimp 'n' Gravy (Gee adds crab to his and recommends ordering a side of it to pour over fish, crab rice, or white rice). His Macaroni & Cheese is derived from an aunt's recipe.

Ironically, it was his white mom, who grew up in Maryland, who taught him to make red rice. She learned the recipe from Virgil's mother. Cooked with tomatoes, onions, and sausage, red rice is "the Blackest thing you can cook," laughs Gee.

The menu has classic soul food dishes such as Greenz (collards) and Poke Chops (fried pork chops). Other items characteristic of the Lowcountry include fried shark bites, shrimp and crab gravy, and lots of seafood.

The Chucktown Chewie Sundae, the only dessert on the menu, features Charleston's famous chewy brown-sugar blondie.

While most of the menu follows tradition, a few dishes are of Gee's invention. His Gullah Egg Rolls are stuffed with red rice, shrimp, and fried cabbage. One of the most popular items is his Slammin' Sammen (blackened Atlantic salmon topped with a crab cream sauce, fried oysters, and shrimp, with white rice and Geechee fried corn).

3721 Main St., College Park
404-228-4897
virgilsgullahkitchen.com

SNACKBOXE BISTRO

Lao street food

Thip Athakhanh and Vanh Sengaphone were both born in Laos but moved to the US as toddlers. Now a couple, they met through mutual friends in Atlanta's Laotian community.

They married in 2016 and honeymooned in Laos—the first time either had returned to the country of their birth.

"Everything about it spoke to us," remembers Thip. "We felt like this is who we are. This is what's been missing." The two knew they wanted to bring Laos to Atlanta.

Later that year, Thip was laid off when the company she worked for went out of business. Vanh had always wanted to own a restaurant, so he encouraged Thip, a talented cook, to hone her culinary skills. For the next two years, she refined her recipes, trying them out on family and friends.

They found a vacant office space in the Super H Mart shopping center in Doraville. To save money, Vanh built out most of the dining room himself while still holding down a full-time day job.

By opening day, word had already gotten out. Atlanta foodies lined up for a first taste. They liked what they ate, evidently; the same year, Thip soon was named "Atlanta's Chef of the Year" by the Atlanta Eater website.

The house specialty is *nam khao*, a zesty, herbaceous, crispy rice salad. Coconut rice is formed into balls, deep fried, and broken into pieces before being tossed with pork, peanuts, lime juice, and herbs.

Laap, the national dish of Laos, is another must. The mincemeat salad is prepared with your choice of beef, tofu, salmon, chicken, or pork belly and mixed with toasted rice powder, kaffir lime leaves, fish sauce, and galangal (a relative of ginger). Order a side of sticky rice, and eat with your fingers.

Left: Their honeymoon was the first time Thip Athakhanh and Vanh Sengaphone returned to their native Laos since their respective childhoods. *Top center:* Get out your camera from the Instagramable Tempura-Fried Squid on a stick. *Above center:* The Charcoaled Lemongrass Ribs are aromatic and tender. *Right:* Mekong Drink blends imported Beerlao with tamarind juice, a tamarind chili flake rim, and a lime wedge.

After Thip's favorite banh mi shop, Quoc Huong, closed during the pandemic, she began offering the classic Vietnamese sandwiches (also found in Laos), featuring her own homemade chicken liver pâté.

The most Instagrammable dish on the menu is the Tempura-Fried Squid on a stick. Thip created the dish as a one-off for an event, but it was such a hit that she added the tempura calamari, topped with tamarind chili flakes, to the menu.

Feeling that the restaurant was missing some of the celebratory spirit of Laos, they added a bar in 2019. Their signature cocktail, Mekong Drink, pairs imported Beerlao with tamarind juice, a tamarind chili flake rim, and a lime wedge.

6035 Peachtree Rd., Ste C114, Doralville
770-417-8082
snackboxebistro.com

In Laos, *khao niew* (sticky rice) is the base of every meal. Order a side of sticky rice and pinch a little in your hand, then use it to pick up bites of each dish. For a beer pairing, try Beerlao, an imported lager from Laos.

R. THOMAS DELUXE GRILL

The quirkiest spot in Buckhead

R. Thomas's pink-and-green-striped, tent-lined walls and its colorful folk art seem out of place among the cookie-cutter strip malls along Peachtree. But that's just the first impression—it gets weirder. Before they reach the door, guests are greeted by cockatoos Peaches and Cream and their feathered friends.

In the 1970s, Richard Bruce Thomas (aka "R. Thomas") was the number-two guy at KFC, second only to the Colonel himself. In 1979, he left to cofound Bojangles, another giant in the fast-food universe. When he sold the business in 1984, he wasn't quite sure what to do with himself, so he traveled the US.

In San Francisco, he stumbled upon Hamburger Mary's, a funky, flamboyant burger joint, which inspired him to create his own quirky burger place in Greenville, South Carolina. This first iteration of R. Thomas didn't survive, and a year later Thomas moved to Atlanta and opened the existing restaurant.

The original menu was handwritten and featured illustrations of every dish. Some menu items (pineapple and vanilla ice cream, served in a cantaloupe, for example) have been retired, while new additions (such as Creole Shrimp Bowl and Mediterranean Bowl) are constantly being added.

In the 1990s, R. had a wake-up call when his new friend healthy-lifestyle evangelist, Donna Gates told him, "You know, you've

> If it feels like you're eating in a tent, it's because you are. The original restaurant had a small footprint, so R. expanded it by adding a covered patio. Today all the seating is technically outdoors in the tented patio, but you can still see the original dining rooms as you wend your way through the kitchen to the bathrooms.

Left: The R. Thomas birds have their own Facebook and Instagram accounts. *Center:* R. Thomas was a fast-food entrepreneur before opening this quirky Buckhead spot. *Top right:* R. Thomas is open 24 hours a day. *Above right:* Southwest chile tortillas are stuffed with chicken, pineapple, fresh basil, red bell pepper, and mandarin oranges for the Chicken Curry Basil Wrap.

poisoned more people in America than drugs have." R. changed his diet and added vegan and raw dishes to the menu.

One night in the late '80s, R. lost the keys to the restaurant. Rather than call a locksmith, he persuaded some staff members to stay the night with him. That evening he discovered that there were people out at all hours looking for someplace to eat. R. Thomas has been open 24 hours a day ever since, creating a popular late-night hangout and attracting all sorts, including a psychic who set up shop at a corner table and told fortunes into the wee hours.

R. received his first parrot, Sparkles, as an egg when he was a lad. Although Sparkles retired to his daughter's house after R. passed in 2017, a menagerie of birds continues to welcome guests. Keep an eye out for Tommy, found in an abandoned building slated for demolition; he has a thing for blondes. And Charlie, the Amazon parrot with a "fowl" mouth, isn't afraid to show off his French before the Sunday morning church crowd.

1812 Peachtree St. NW
404-881-0246
rthomasdeluxegrill.net

STARLIGHT DRIVE-IN FLEA MARKET

Now showing: Mexican street food

Every night, folks pull into Atlanta' only drive-in theater for a double feature and typical movie theater fare—popcorn, nachos, and candy. But on weekends from 6 a.m. to 3 p.m. the Starlight is transformed into a flea market—and there you'll find some of the best Mexican street food in the city.

As soon as you enter, you'll notice fellow customers with plates piled high with *chicharrones de harina*. Also known as *pasta para duros* (hard paste), these bright orange pinwheels puff up when deep fried, resulting in a light, airy consistency similar to cheese puffs or pork rinds. The pinwheels are sold either in a plastic bag, tossed with lime juice and hot sauce, or on a plate, topped with shredded lettuce, onions, lime juice, and hot sauce.

Work up an appetite while exploring rows of cleaning supplies, cosmetics, paper products, shoes, clothing, toys, electronics, and what-have-you. You'll find sneakers to die for, every type of tool imaginable, and piles of naked Barbies. Wade through boxes of seasonal items that once graced Target shelves, scratch-and-dent items from CVS, and brand-name finds at deep discounts.

Just don't let avarice distract your appetite. The real attraction at the Starlight Drive-In is the chow!

Stop by tables lined with huge plastic jugs full of *agua frescos* (fruit juices) of every color; tubs of *dulces* (Mexican candy); and sliced mangos, pineapples and papaya, waiting to be topped with chili powder and lime juice. You may want to bring dental floss in case you want to dig into the *elote*—corn on the cob drenched in cotija cheese, mayonnaise, chili powder, and lime juice.

Left: Flea market shoppers line up at Santiago's Mexican Taqueria, one of the regular food trucks. *Center:* Listen for the bell of the *paletas* (popsicle) cart. *Top right:* Mexican street-style tacos are cheap and delicious at the drive-in. *Above right: Elote*—corn on the cob on a stick covered in cotija cheese, mayonnaise, chili powder, and lime juice. Photos by Stephen Nowland.

Listen closely for a bell, the tell-tale sound of the *paletas* (popsicle) cart. If the food gods are with you, you'll run into vendors selling *tortas* (Mexican sandwiches) or *tamales* (corn dough stuffed with meat, cheese, or veggies, steamed inside a corn husk).

Nothing beats the tacos on sale at the Starlight: corn tortillas filled with your choice of meat and topped with chopped white onions and cilantro. One food truck even has a toppings cart stocked with salsas, lime wedges, hot peppers, and pickled carrots.

In addition to the prepared foods, Mexican staples, including huge *nopalitos* (cactus paddles), tomatillos, cilantro, masa, tortillas, and produce needed for a delicious dinner, are offered by different vendors.

At half a buck, the price of admission, your day at the Starlight *mercado al aire libra* (open air market) may be the best bargain you'll find in Atlanta.

Saturdays and Sundays from 6 a.m to 3 p.m.
2000 Moreland Ave.
starlightdrivein.com

Street Taco Lexicon

Al pastor: sautéed pork marinated in lemon and pineapple juice
Asada: grilled steak
Pollo: chicken
Barbacoa: shredded beef

Chorizo: spicy Mexican sausage
Carnitas: diced pork
Lengua: beef tongue
Suadero: beef from below the breast bone

CAFÉ INTERMEZZO

A European coffeehouse in the heart of Atlanta

For some people, there is one moment in their life that changes everything. For Brian Olson, it was the first time he stepped inside a German *konditorei*.

It was 1971. Brian was 21 and traveling across Europe for the first time. He had never seen this type of coffeehouse, with its wood-paneled walls, brass chandeliers, bountiful pastry case display, and shiny brass espresso machine. But the thing that touched his soul was the spirit of the café. Patrons might stop by for a quick coffee or spend hours reading the paper, writing in their journals, or discussing current events with other guests. Brian knew he needed to introduce the US to this European coffeehouse culture.

Returning to Minneapolis, where he grew up, Brian gained restaurant experience and started a career as a traveling salesperson, selling espresso machines to restaurants and cafés around the Midwest. Looking for a larger sales territory, Brian moved to Atlanta in 1977. Wherever he went, he took a notebook for jotting down ideas for the coffeehouse he hoped to open one day—learning from the mistakes and successes of restaurants he visited.

In 1979, he learned of a new shopping center under construction in Dunwoody. He opened the original Café Intermezzo in Park Place, where it's still going strong. Over 40 years later, there are several Café Intermezzos in the metro area as well as cafés in Dallas and Nashville.

Walking into Café Intermezzo feels like stepping into another world. The wood paneling, brass chandeliers, and candlelight

> Ask for a dollop of *schlag* (whipped cream) to top any dessert or coffee drink.

Left: Brian Olson designed his signature espresso machine, a combination of two machines. *Top center:* The pastry case at Café Intermezzo is the stuff dreams are made of. *Bottom center:* Café Intermezzo is the perfect spot for a romantic dessert date. *Right:* Brian Olson created Café Intermezzo to bring the European coffeehouse vibe to Atlanta.

contribute to the romantic atmosphere. The imposing brass espresso machine (which Brian designed by combining two machines) is glamorously whimsical. But the pièces de résistance are pastry cases filled with more than 20 kinds of pastries and desserts. The Dunwoody and Peachtree locations each have two cases, giving guests an overwhelming choice of 40 cheesecakes, tortes, and other delicacies.

There's a full menu, but it's overshadowed by the 65-page beverage book, chock-full of coffee drinks, hot chocolates, teas, and cocktails. The beverage book is more than a menu. It's a textbook that explains every coffee, tea, liquor, wine, and beer served.

It's the perfect spot for a date, a celebration, or a cup of coffee. Channeling the spirit of a European coffeehouse, guests are encouraged to stay as long as they like.

"I want guests to savor the environment and relish the moment," says Brian, who believes that each visit to Café Intermezzo can be a mini-vacation from life's drudgeries. "It's a step into another time, another place."

Midtown:	4505 Ashford Dunwoody Rd.,	100 Avalon Blvd.,
1065 Peachtree St., Ste. 2	Dunwoody	Alpharetta
404-355-0411	770-396-1344	470-322-4202

cafeintermezzo.com

MAMAK

From the streets of Malaysia

At age 18, Wong Wai Lee went to work in his older brother's dim sum restaurant. They both were born and grew up in Malaysia, and the restaurant reflected the family's Chinese heritage.

Wai Lee continued in the restaurant industry until, at age 31, he moved to New York City. He hoped to work as a chef, but he didn't speak English, lacked connections in the industry, and definitely didn't have the funds to open his own restaurant. So for the next decade and a half, he had a variety of jobs, including washing dishes, working at an industrial laundry, and selling wholesale groceries.

After 9/11, Wai Lee had difficulty finding work. He moved to Atlanta where he had family, including his nephew Alan Foong, who was looking for a chef for the Malaysian restaurant he owned. Finally, Chef Wong was back in the kitchen.

For the next 13 years he worked in a number of Chinese and Malaysian restaurants around the city, until he came across a tiny storefront in a strip mall on Buford Highway. The space wasn't much to speak of, but it was affordable. Chef Wong could imagine cooking up homemade Malaysian dishes in the modest space.

So he talked to his nephew Alan, and, in 2014, they opened Mamak, which means "food stall."

With Malay, Chinese, and Indian influences, Malaysian cuisine reflects the multiethnic makeup of the nation's population. The Indian influence, for example, can be seen in *roti canai* (a crispy Indian flatbread served with a chicken potato curry dipping sauce) and assorted curries.

Mamak serves up the most popular Malaysian dishes, including Chow Kway Teow (wok-fried flat rice noodles tossed with shrimp, squid, egg, bean sprouts, soy sauce, and chili paste—popular in

Left: Mamak and Mamak Vegan Kitchen serve up Malaysian street food dishes. *Top center:* No longer a simple hole-in-the-wall on Buford Highway, Mamak has moved to more elegant digs. *Above center:* Olive Fried Rice dish from Mamak Vegan Kitchen—wok-tossed fried rice, olive leaves, carrots, stringbeans, tofu, and ginger. *Right:* Chef Wong Wai Lee has been cooking since he was 18.

Penang), Curry Laksa (a spicy noodle soup made with coconut milk, curry, and noodles, served with your choice of chicken or spare ribs), and Hainanese Chicken (a deceptively simple dish of poached chicken served with a sweet ginger-chili dipping sauce, chili oil, and fragrant rice that was cooked with chicken broth).

In addition to traditional dishes, Chef Wong has created new dishes that cater to American palates. He replaced the fish heads on the menu with fish fillets. Mamak Chicken is his take on General Tso's Chicken, but spicier.

In 2020, Mamak moved to a larger space with contemporary design elements and opened Mamak Vegan Kitchen, a plant-based concept, next door.

2390 Chamblee Tucker Rd., Ste 101,
Chamblee
470-375-3190
mamak-kitchen.com

2390 Chamblee Tucker Rd.,
Chamblee
678-909-8188
mamakvegan.com

To spice up your dishes, ask your server for a side of sambal (a homemade chili paste) or pickled green chilies (sour and slightly spicy, house-pickled jalapeños).

TICONDEROGA CLUB

Your membership awaits

Greg Best, Regan Smith, Paul Calvert, David Bies, and Bart Sasso had something in common. All veterans of the food and beverage industry, they envisioned one of two likely futures: either join a restaurant group and spend years clawing their way up the management ladder, or open a place of their own and work 24/7 as a chef/owner. Neither path appealed to them.

So the five of them spent more than a year meeting weekly to workshop ideas. They deconstructed the very concept of a restaurant, deciding their place would be a sandbox for testing new ideas. Necessary elements were keeping the guest experience top priority while also creating a sustainable and fulfilling career path for the partners and their staff. Ticonderoga Club is the result.

As guests enter Ticonderoga Club, nestled in the far corner of Krog Street Market, they enter a different world and time. Instead of the bustling, fluorescent lit food hall, they find themselves in a New England tavern of a bygone era. Everyone may not know you by name, but you feel like they ought to.

By merely opening the menu, you agree to the terms and conditions of a lifetime membership to Ticonderoga Club. The name itself evokes feelings of warmth, the familiarity of shared experiences—perhaps a bull session after a rugby match or a spirited campfire on the final night of summer camp. Wherever your mind takes you, it will be a long way from Atlanta.

> Seeking a late-night snack? Before the kitchen closes each night, they prepare plenty of bacon, egg, and cheese sandwiches. Just ask for a Yankee. But, never go on Wednesday. The Club never opens on Wednesdays.

Top left: The Ipswich Clam Roll is a menu staple. *Bottom left:* The Captain's Chair is the most coveted seat at the bar. *Top right:* Each night before the kitchen closes, they make a stack of BECs (bacon, egg, and cheese sandwiches) for the late-night crowd. *Bottom right:* Ticonderoga Cup—Plantation 5 Year Rum, brandy, sherry, lemon, and pineapple. Photo by Mia Yakel.

David, the chef, cut his teeth at Restaurant Eugene. He has created a serendipitous menu with pub favorites listed along with comfort foods inspired by his travels to Asia as well as Central and South America. A Japanese-inspired steak tartare competes for your approval with Cobb salad or fish & chips. Although the menu is frequently revised, certain Club classics, including the Ipswich Clam Roll, are menu fixtures.

For a communal dining experience, order the Chuck Wagon Dinner, a 48-ounce black angus chuck roast served with fresh horseradish and sides. This order leaves the kitchen with boisterous fanfare—bell ringing, hooting, and hollering.

With three all-stars of Atlanta's craft cocktail scene (Greg, Regan, and Paul), Ticonderoga Club boasts one of Atlanta's most celebrated beverage menus.

Arrive early to score the Captain's Chair, the boat seat installed in honor of Regan's father, an avid fisherman who passed away before the Club opened.

Krog Street Market
99 Krog St. NE
404-458-4534
ticonderogaclub.com

WE SUKI SUKI

EAV's micro global food hall

We Suki Suki is the quintessential hole-in-the-wall. The galley kitchen takes up most of the tiny storefront, leaving little room for customers to order at the counter. And there are always customers. Quynh (Q) Trinh's BBQ Pork, Lemongrass Chicken, Asian Eggplant, Local Tofu, and Classic Dac Biet (pâté and deli cuts) Banh Mi are East Atlanta favorites.

So it's not surprising that when the adjacent storefront was vacant, Q snatched it up. Finally, guests would have a place to slurp their pho and sip their bubble tea!

But Q had other plans for the space.

As an entrepreneur, she knew how difficult it could be for would-be restaurateurs to break into the industry. Without capital or financial backers, it's next to impossible to afford a brick-and-mortar space. Q saw an opportunity to create an incubator for new food businesses.

The Global Grub Collective is a micro food hall, home to a rotating cast of vendors. For some, it's a short-term location until they grow their business enough to get their own space. Others have found a permanent home in the food hall.

Poke Burri locations are popping up around the country, but the original is still inside the Global Grub Collective. They take poke to the next level with spicy tuna nachos, sushi burrito rolls, and sushi donuts.

Best known for their warm, fluffy *baos* (steamed buns) stuffed with anything from cauliflower to duck confit, Mushi Ni also serves *roti cakes* (Malaysian flatbread), bowls, and Tokyo fries (tossed in umami spices and served with a truffle sriracha mayo).

Marrakech Express serves Moroccan dishes such as Lamb Tanjiya (bone-in lamb shank slow-cooked with garlic, cumin, and preserved lemon) and Chicken Shawarma Bowl (marinated chicken with rice, green beans, hummus, beet salad, and green salad).

Left: Chef Amal cooks up authentic Moroccan and Mediterranean cuisine at Marrakech Express. *Middle:* Xen Renal's Pakistani Bun Kabab is lamb patty topped with a fried egg and tamarind chutney. *Top right:* Guests line up for Quynh (Q) Trinh's BBQ Pork, Lemongrass Chicken, Asian Eggplant, Local Tofu, and Classic Dac Biet (pâté and deli cuts) Banh Mi. *Bottom right:* Poke Burri takes a playful approach to sushi with their Sushi Donut.

During summer, you can find Xen Renai creating Xenwiches (global-inspired sandwiches) such as Pakistani Bun Kebab (lamb patty, fried egg, and tamarind chutney on a burger bun) or Argentinian Choripan (chorizo paired with a cilantro lime chimichurri on French bread).

Brock's Comfort Zone serves such Southern favorites as Shrimp and Grits and Ho Cakes.

A bowl of ramen from Lifting Noodle is the perfect antidote for a cold night.

The Afro-Latin Zun Zun EAV! serves Caribbean favorites: Cuban sandwiches, rice & bean bowls, tostones, and empanadas.

The vendors may change from day to day and month to month, but each stall overflows with unique personality and flavor.

477 Flat Shoals Rd.
wesukisuki.com

Vendors set their own hours, so check online to make sure your favorites are open before heading over. Or just show up and see who's cooking what when you get there! Seating at the picnic tables is limited, so plan on sharing a table.

HAVANA SANDWICH SHOP

Buford highway pioneer

After the Cuban Revolution, 11-year-old Eddie Benedit was sent to Atlanta to live with his aunt and uncle. He and his brother came to the US on student visas sponsored by the Catholic Church. His parents, Guido and Estrella, joined them a year later.

In December 1975, he married Atlanta native Debbie Matrangos. On their way home from their honeymoon in Miami, Eddie announced he planned to open a Cuban sandwich shop.

"Who in the #%&$ will eat Cuban food in Atlanta?" asked Debbie. Not to mention that Eddie had no restaurant experience.

Down the street from the newlyweds' Buford Highway apartment was a Christmas tree lot. Eddie persuaded the owner to let him rent the small building on the property. They signed the lease December 31, 1975. With the help of the entire family, the Havana Sandwich Shop opened less than six weeks later on February 9, 1976.

It's credited as the first immigrant-owned restaurant on Buford Highway, now known as Atlanta's mecca for international cuisine.

Cuban Sandwiches sold for $1, and Cokes were a quarter.

Eddie managed the kitchen while his father and Debbie ran the front of the house. Estrella contributed her flan and rice pudding recipes. Many nights, Eddie or Guido slept on a cot in the back to get an early start the next morning.

Item No. 17 (a half Cuban with a side of black beans, yellow rice, and rojo sauce) is by far the most popular dish on the menu. Ask for some extra mojo for your Cuban sandwich! Though it's not on the menu, you can ask for a vegetarian Cuban, in which the meats are replaced with grilled mojo-marinated mushrooms, onions, and green peppers.

Left: The No. 17—a half Cuban with a side of black beans, yellow rice, and rojo sauce. *Center:* Eddie Benedit (*below*) and his father Guido (*above*) poured themselves into the new restaurant, often sleeping in the back office. *Right:* Along the walls of this no-frills dining room you'll find family momentos, which survived the fire.

The Benedits couldn't find authentic Cuban bread in Atlanta, so they shipped it in from Tampa. Even those rolls weren't fresh enough, so they switched to French rolls until they found a local baker, Mr. Garcia, who could bake Cuban bread.

Their Cuban sandwich follows tradition (yellow mustard, thinly sliced ham, mojo-marinated pork, and pickles on Cuban bread) except for one ingredient. Instead of Swiss cheese, Eddie preferred white American, because it melts well and the taste is less overwhelming.

Eddie, who has since passed away, was meticulous with his recipes. For instance, he never flavored his black beans with meat, and he insisted on Hunt's tomato sauce in his rojo sauce. Some of today's kitchen crew trained under Eddie, and they still do things his way.

Debbie and her eldest son, Eddie Jr., who grew up in the sandwich shop, run the restaurant today.

In 2008, the Havana Sandwich Shop suffered a devastating fire. For years, the sandwich shop operated in a strip mall up the road, but they reopened in the original location in 2015.

2905 Buford Hwy. NE
404-636-4094
Havanaatlanta.com

Where everybody knows your name, honey

Sometimes you go to a restaurant because you want to try something new. Sometimes you decide you want the tried and true. For the latter, head to the Colonnade.

The original version opened in 1927, on the corner of Piedmont Road and Lindbergh Drive. The restaurant relocated to Cheshire Bridge Road in 1972.

Fortunately for the Colonnade's loyal patrons, successive owners have valued tradition. When the third owner, Jack Clark, decided to sell in 1979, he took out an ad, inviting would-be buyers to submit an essay.

Paul Jones, who had moved to Atlanta five years earlier to manage the Cherokee Country Club, was in the market for his own restaurant. He brought his nine-year-old daughter, Jodi, along to check it out.

"I couldn't figure out why all these ladies were calling my dad 'Honey,' if he'd never been there before," Jodi remembers.

But before Jack Clark would sell, he insisted on taking a road trip with Paul to his hometown in Michigan to meet his family. Only after seeing where Paul grew up, did Jack feel confident the Colonnade would be in good hands.

Today, Jodi and her husband run the restaurant. Much remains the same, including the staff. Sonya, the head cook, has been in the kitchen for more than 40 years, Randell Stenson has been greeting guests for 30 years, and Rhea Merritt has been at the Colonnade since 1972.

The menu has changed little. At any other restaurant, you would be hard-pressed to find Tomato Aspic (Bloody Mary mix, onions, celery, and gelatin, with a side of mayonnaise) or Pear and Cheese (canned Bartlett pears, shredded cheddar cheese, and a side of mayonnaise) on the menu.

Left: The Colonnade is one of those iconic places you need to try at least once. *Top center:* The Tomato Aspic (a savory, Bloody Mary–inspired jelly) is a throwback to the 1950s. *Bottom center:* Like every good Southern restaurant, the Colonnade is known for its fried chicken. *Top right:* The Coconut Iced Box Pie and other desserts are made in-house. *Bottom right:* You'll know you're home when you see the neon sign at the Colonnade. All photos by George Gussin.

The Southern fried chicken is the most popular entree. Other favorites include Roasted Turkey Breast (with celery dressing, giblet gravy, and cranberry sauce) and A Lot of Livers (fried or boiled chicken livers).

Jodi says she doesn't dare change the menu for fear of a patrons' revolt.

The Marian Salad is named for a regular customer who always asked for chopped tomatoes and red onions on her salad. Other regulars would order a "Marian," so Jodi added it to the menu, where it remains today as a tribute to the beloved patron, since passed.

Regulars, affectionately described as "gay and gray," consider the Colonnade their country club. Many patrons will drop by several times a week. Some come every day.

1879 Cheshire Bridge Rd. NE
404-874-5642
thecolonnadeatlanta.com

Dining alone? Find a spot at the bar. The Colonnade is known for strong pours and friendly customers. You won't be alone for long.

CENTRAL FOOD HALL AT PCM

Fresh tastes in historic Ponce City Market

Driving down Ponce de Leon, it's impossible to miss Ponce City Market (PCM). The 2.1-million-square-foot brick building was constructed in 1926 as the regional headquarters for Sears, Roebuck and Co. The City of Atlanta bought the massive structure in 1990, and for two decades, it was known as "City Hall East."

Today, PCM is a mixed-use development with offices, residential units, retail stores, restaurants, and the giant Central Food Hall.

Anne Quatrano's Bacchanalia (see page 4) has long been considered the pinnacle of fine dining in Atlanta, but at PCM, the restaurateur reinvented the fish camp experience with W. H. Stiles Fish Camp. Traditional seafood favorites such as lobster rolls, crab cakes, and fish & chips are served along with New Orleans-inspired po'boys, catfish paired with flavors of Vietnam, and crispy squid in a Korean vinaigrette.

For years, Holeman & Finch (see page 42) sold 24 burgers a night, available only after 10 p.m. Today, you can score the renowned burgers anytime at H&F Burger. Next door is another concept by Chef Linton Hopkins, Hop's Chicken, specializing in fried chicken biscuits.

Sean Brock's Minero offers Mexican-inspired fare and craft cocktails, and Hector Santiago serves Latin-inspired sandwiches at El Super Pan (see page 130).

Although some restaurants have their own dining rooms and patios, most of the seating is in the communal dining area on the first or second floors. After picking up food from your favorite stall, stop by the Tap on Ponce for a glass draft beer or wine to go with your meal.

Left: Ponce City Market was built in 1926 as a distribution center for Sears, Roebuck and Co. *Center:* On weekends, it can be tricky to find an empty table at the Central Food Hall. *Right:* Many restaurants in the Central Food Hall also have outdoor dining areas. Photos courtesy of PCM.

At Botiwalla, the team behind Chai Pani (see page 118) reimagines Indian street food—Lamb Sliders, Masala Smashed Potatoes, and Paneer Tikka Rolls.

Bellina Alimentari offers not only Italian dishes but also imported ingredients and cooking classes.

And that's just the start. PCM offers Mediterranean, South African, and Szechuan cuisines, among others.

Head to the second floor for freshly baked breads from Root Baking Co., which mills heirloom grains in-house, or order an artisan cocktail at Likewise, inside Citizen Supply.

Hints of PCM's past are everywhere—from architectural remnants to the names of some vendors. Spiller Park Coffee honors the former Ponce de Leon Ballpark, which was right across the street. Nicknamed Spiller Park, for R. J. Spiller (who commissioned the park), it was home to two minor-league teams, the Atlanta Crackers and the Atlanta Black Crackers, from 1907 to 1964.

Located on the roof, Skyline Park is a reference to the Ponce de Leon amusement park, which once occupied the site. Smoked turkey legs, foot-long frankfurters, funnel cakes, and other carnival favorites are available.

Named for Atlanta's second electric street car, the Nine Mile Circle Ride, 9 Mile Station serves up incredible rooftop views of downtown, Midtown, and Buckhead. For a more upscale experience, 12 Cocktail Bar offers small plates, classic cocktails, and rare spirits.

675 Ponce de Leon Ave. NE
404-900-7900
poncecitymarket.com

LITTLE'S FOOD STORE

The heart of Cabbagetown

To fully appreciate Little's, you first should know about Cabbagetown. The former mill village was established in 1881 for workers at the Fulton Bag and Cotton Mill. The mill owned the two-story shotgun and cottage-style houses and leased them to white laborers who migrated from the Appalachian region of north Georgia to work in the factory.

In 1929, the Little family opened a corner grocery store for the people in the neighborhood. The shelves along the walls were won by Mrs. Little in a contest sponsored by the IGA (Independent Grocers Alliance).

Over the years, Cabbagetown underwent a series of transformations. Even before the mill closed in 1978, musicians and artists had moved in as harbingers of gentrification. Rents and housing prices skyrocketed while mom-and-pop stores floundered. Of 10 independent groceries that once served Cabbagetown, only Little's remains.

To survive, the store had to evolve as well. In 1969, the Littles' son, Leon, took over the store and added a lunch counter and a grill. Soon, his burgers, egg salad sandwiches, and lime sours were keeping the doors open.

In 2006, Leon sold the store to Lisa Hanson, who remade it into Cabbagetown Market and Grill, a gourmet market. Little's hamburgers remained, but were joined by such exotic fare as banh mi, muffulettas, and Cuban sandwiches.

Four years later, Brad and Nina Cunard took over the lease for the rechristened Little's Food Store. Once again, the tiny store reflects the spirit of Cabbagetown. Neighbors run in to pick up a bottle of wine or an onion needed to complete a dinner recipe, but stay to catch up with neighbors. The late-night crowd stops in for a burger

Left: The tiny storefront is easy to miss. *Top center:* The original wooden shelves Mrs. Little won in a contest can be seen all around the store. *Above center:* The Little Burgers are 2 ounces each, compared to the 4-ounce patties of the Big Burgers. *Right:* Vintage memorabilia and folk art by local artists show Little's connection to the neighborhood.

or a six-pack. Brad greets customers by name and often reaches for their favorite brand of cigarettes before they have time to ask.

"Little's is known as the heart of the neighborhood," explains Brad. "It already was. All we had to do was not mess it up."

Though Little's continues to evolve, respect for its roots are everywhere you look. The shelves Mrs. Little won are still in place, as is the counter Leon installed. Behind the counter is a display case filled with memorabilia from "Old Atlanta," and the walls are lined with work by local artists.

With only eight counter seats and one four-top, most food is served to-go. If you get lucky, snag a seat at the counter and take in the sights.

198 Carroll St.
404-963-7012
littlesfoodstore.com

Stop by in the morning for a pork sausage, egg, and cheese biscuit. Both the sausage and biscuits are prepared from scratch. Not super hungry? Order a Little Burger. The 2-ounce patties make a great (and cheap) snack! Although not on the menu, you can usually order a fried chicken sandwich.

DELIA'S CHICKEN SAUSAGE STAND

What the cluck?

D elia Champion is a third-generation restaurateur. "It's all I know," she says. As a child in New Jersey, her family lived above the family bar. By age five, she was grilling onions, standing on a chair to reach the stove. She can still remember her grandfather and father grinding pheasant and venison to make their own sausage.

After moving to Atlanta in the '70s, Delia spent years working front of house in restaurants, until she and some friends opened the Flying Biscuit in Candler Park in 1993.

When Flying Biscuit (see page 116) first opened, they didn't serve pork because they wanted to serve the type of food they preferred. Instead, they offered turkey sausage, but Delia was dissatisfied with the texture. During downtime, they would experiment with different ingredients. Duck and Grand Mariner were a surprisingly good combination, blueberries did not make the grade, and so on.

Finally, they settled on ground chicken with sage and a little cayenne pepper for kick. While most breakfast restaurants offered bacon or pork sausage, chicken sausage and soysage were the only options at Flying Biscuit.

After selling the Flying Biscuit, Delia focused on the chicken sausage. Her first breakthrough was with a grocery store on

> The popular meatball hoagie is no longer on the menu, but they'll make it if you ask. Vegetarian options are available for the slingers and sliders—just say, "cluck off." Looking for something sweet to finish off your meal? Try a Cake Shake: a milkshake blended with a homemade cupcake!

Left: Delia Champion perfected her chicken sausage recipe at her first restaurant, the Flying Biscuit. *Center:* The Hot Mess Combo—link chicken sausage topped with chili, cheddar cheese, and pickled jalapenos, with a side of Wedgies. *Right:* Both locations are open 24 hours on weekends.

Bankhead Highway that agreed to sell her sausage and let her perform in-store demonstrations to garner interest. Soon her sausage was being sold in Publix and Kroger stores across Atlanta.

In 2011, Delia opened her first chicken-sausage stand in a modest location, tucked among fast-food restaurants on Moreland Avenue. Her restaurant offers ultra-casual food, cooked to order. Delia hopes hungry people on their way to McDonald's will decide to stop at her chicken sausage stand instead. If so, their taste buds—if not their lives—will be forever changed.

The original menu listed two types of dishes: Slingers (a jumbo chicken sausage link in a hoagie) and Sliders (chicken sausage patties on a soft bun). Over the years, a number of specials, including meatloaf and lasagna, have found a permanent home on the menu.

The East Atlanta eatery has been joined by the Westside location and four stands at the Mercedes-Benz Stadium. Three of the stands serve the Hot Mess (link chicken sausage, chili, cheddar cheese, and pickled jalapeños) and the Prime Time (chicken sausage, onions, pepper, and comeback sauce—a stadium exclusive). If you are fortunate enough to find the fourth stand, reward yourself with the Chickie Philly Classic.

East Atlanta:
489 Moreland Ave. SE
404-474-9651

Westside:
881 Marietta St. NW
404-254-0408

thesausagestand.com

GU'S DUMPLINGS & GU'S KITCHEN

Numbingly delicious

As a child in Chengdu, a Szechuan province in southwestern China, Yiquan Gu aspired to become a chef. At age 15, he began studying under a master chef, but before he was allowed to chop his first vegetable, he had to spend two years washing dishes. Eventually, the master decided he'd taught Gu everything he could and told his protégé it was time to create his own path.

Yiquan moved to the US to help a cousin manage a struggling restaurant and quickly developed a reputation for flipping unsuccessful restaurants. He traveled the country, consulting and training chefs.

In 2010, Chef Gu received a call from a restaurateur on Buford Highway who asked Gu to take over his lease. Yiquan and his wife, Qiongyao Zhang, agreed that it was time to have a restaurant of their own.

On their first day, they served a total of two customers. The location, tucked into a strip mall, was only part of the problem. The traditional Szechuan menu appealed to Chinese palates, but such exotic dishes as pork intestine and frog turned off non-Asian customers. Word eventually spread, however, and business skyrocketed following a favorable mention in *Atlanta Magazine*.

Dumplings were the top seller. Customers would stop their daughter, Yvonne, from clearing their plates until they had sopped up

> Don't miss the handmade Sweet and Spicy Thick Noodles, created daily. Numbing Szechuan peppercorn powder adds a kick to the Szechuan Tofu Po'boy, a New Orleans–inspired vegetarian sandwich.

Left: The spicy Zhong-Style Dumplings should not be missed. *Center:* The Gu family on a rare day off: Qiongyao Zhang, Yvonne Gu Khan, and Chef Yiquan Gu. *Right:* Homemade Sweet and Spicy Thick Noodles.

the last drop of the spicy sauce. "I could eat my shoe with this sauce," one guest exclaimed.

Yvonne proposed that the family open a second concept—a stand at Krog Street Market—that would serve a limited menu of dumplings and a few other best-sellers. It was a hit.

When their lease for Gu's Bistro came up for renewal, the landlord pushed for a long-term lease. Business was booming at both locations, but Yiquan and Qiongyao were getting older and were ready to slow down.

Five years after opening Gu's Bistro, the family closed their original restaurant to focus on Gu's Dumplings. One afternoon, Gu called Yvonne during his drive home, "This is the first time in 15 years that I'm going home while the sun is out."

But the family is back at it. In 2018 and 2019, they opened two new restaurants: Gu's Kitchen (Szechuan street food in a casual atmosphere) in Atlanta, and a second Gu's Dumplings in Alpharetta.

When he can, Yiquan Gu returns to China to visit his mentor, who must be proud of his protégé.

Gu's Dumplings

Krog Street Market:
99 Krog St. NE
404-527-6007

6330 Halcyon Way, Alpharetta
678-691-4844
gusdumplings.com

Gu's Kitchen
4897 Buford Hwy., Chamblee
470-299-2388
guskitchen.com

XOCOLATL SMALL BATCH CHOCOLATE

Gourmet chocolate microfactory

Elaine Read and Matt Weyandt met in 2004 while door-knocking for the DNC. Disillusioned with the outcome of the election, they moved to Panama. After a few months they wanted to keep exploring, so they backpacked across Central America until their money ran out—but not before falling in love with Puerto Viejo, a quiet Costa Rican town. Over the years, they fantasized about moving to Puerto Viejo, but it never felt like the time was right.

Fast forward to 2012: Matt was finishing up a stint with Congressman John Lewis's primary campaign, and Elaine was pregnant with their second child. Feeling burned out, Matt finally decided it was the right time for them to move to Costa Rica.

Once again, money was tight. Their sole luxury each week was a locally made chocolate bar. Made from only two ingredients (cacao and cane sugar), this dark delicacy was unlike anything either had tasted back home.

"It tasted fundamentally different than any chocolate I'd grown up eating," remembers Elaine. "It felt healthier, like a substantial food."

On a tour of a cacao farm and chocolate factory, the couple learned two key facts: one, like wine or coffee, chocolate's taste varies according to the variety of the raw produce, the region where—in the case of cacao beans—it's grown, and how it's processed; two, the processing could be done anywhere, including Atlanta!

Matt apprenticed with local chocolatiers, so by the end of 2013, when their savings were depleted, they headed home armed with a 50-pound bag of cacao beans and a rudimentary but expanding knowledge of how to make chocolate.

Left: Elaine Read and Matt Weyandt roll up their sleeves in their Krog Street Market microfactory. *Right:* Xocolatl Small Batch chocolate bars are made right in Krog Street Market.

Matt and Elaine still weren't sure whether Atlantans would ante-up for handcrafted, single-origin dark chocolate bars that were several times costlier than the chocolate they were accustomed to. To their surprise—and delight—customers at the 2014 Inman Park Festival, where they introduced their chocolate, bought their entire inventory and demanded more. That same year, Matt and Elaine opened their micro-factory and retail store in Krog Street Market, where their chocolate continues to earn rave reviews.

One of their first flavors, the Soul Rebel, remains one of their most popular. It features their own Jamaican jerk spice blend, including thyme, scorpion pepper, and coconut milk. For an intense taste, try the Pure 100%—a bar of pure Nicaraguan cacao with no added sugar or sweeteners.

Krog Street Market:
99 Krog St. NE
404-333-8562
xocolatlchocolate.com

To see how the chocolate gets made, sign up for a tour and tasting of their micro-factory in Krog Street Market. Want to share a bar with a long distance friend? Xocolatl ships nationwide.

THE SILVER SKILLET

It's not retro. It's original.

If you feel like you're stepping into a time warp when you walk into the Silver Skillet, you aren't mistaken.

From the terra-cotta and avocado booths to boomerang patterns on the chrome and Formica tables, every detail dates from 1956 or thereabouts. The handwritten menu signs hanging over the lunch counter are original. No one's taken down the pictures of horses the original owner hung for his daughter. Little has changed at the Silver Skillet, and therein lies its charm.

During the '50s, Tommy Haygood spent summers cooking in the Poconos, and then would shift to Florida kitchens for the winter season. Wearying of the biannual migration, he split the distance and opened a diner in Atlanta not far from the interstate.

Tommy hired Jimmy Collins, who attended Georgia Tech for a short time before pursuing his love of designing commercial kitchens, to design the Skillet. From the angled shark fin windows to the layout of the booths, Jimmy brought Tommy's dreams to life. He fought Tommy on his decision to save money by putting the bathrooms in the kitchen. Jim lost that fight, so to this day, guests must exit the restaurant proper, then enter the kitchen through an external door to reach the restrooms. (Jimmy, incidentally, went on to become president of Chick-fil-A, where you don't have to go outside to reach the bathroom.)

For the most part, the Deckers, who have owned the Silver Skillet since 1967, have changed little at this vintage diner.

Open for breakfast and lunch, the Silver Skillet offers such Southern classics as Country Ham Steak with Red Eye Gravy, Country Fried Steak, and Fried Chicken.

Kids are the first to notice the candy display by the register, but the parents and grandparents are even more tickled to find such

Left: At first glance, the Silver Skillet is a throwback to the 1950s. *Top right:* From the terracotta and avocado color scheme to the chrome and Formica tables, everything at the Skillet is original. *Above right:* The Skillet Country Ham with Red Eye Gravy comes with two eggs, grits, and toast or biscuits.

childhood favorites as Black Jack gum and candy cigarettes for sale alongside sweets of more recent vintages.

Customers aren't the only ones who revel in this blast from the past. The Silver Skillet tops lists of movie locations for scouts looking for a '50s-era diner as a set for movies, television shows, or commercials. Among the productions in which this storied eatery appears are *Remember the Titans*, *Ozark*, and *Anchorman 2*.

The homemade Lemon Ice-Box pie George Decker added to the menu was voted one of the "5 Best Pies in the USA" by *Life Magazine*, and, in 2012, *Saveur* magazine named it one of the "Top 100 Foods in the World."

200 14th St. NW
404-874-1388
thesilverskillet.com

The famous Skillet country ham is pretty salty, so you may want to ask your server for a sample before committing.

BIG DAVE'S CHEESESTEAK

Better than Philly

Two men had a huge impact on Derrick "D" Hayes's life. Years later, he's still paying forward their love, and Atlanta's the better for it.

During high school, following his parent's separation, D moved from West Philadelphia to Athens, Georgia, to live with his grandparents. His grandfather taught him to cook soul food with his special mix of spices.

When D was 22, his father, Big Dave, was diagnosed with lung cancer. He died within six months.

A serious accident left D suffering from physical and emotional damage, including depression and an addiction to painkillers. After moving to Atlanta, D quickly blew through his savings.

In 2014, he used the last of the money to open a small "water ice" shop in a Dunwoody Shell station. He soon realized that most of his customers were unfamiliar with the frozen dessert that was so popular in Philadelphia. He retooled the concept focusing on Philly cheesesteaks with the goal to make them "better than Philly."

For the first few months, the food was fair, but it was not Philly.

D closed the restaurant for three weeks to take care of his sick grandfather. Before he passed, he told D two things: "You're going to be okay," and "Use a little water."

Following his grandfather's advice on the proper ratio of water to oil for dousing the flat top stove surface, D was able to cut down on

> The cheesesteaks are HUGE, so come hungry or split one with a friend. For a smaller, less messy option, the deep-fried Cheesesteak Egg Rolls are must. There are no vegetarian items on the menu, but pescatarians and meat-eaters alike love the Salmon Cheesesteaks and Egg Rolls.

Left: When you bite into a Cheesesteak Eggroll, you're left wondering where it's been all your life. *Center:* Derrick "D" Hayes was inspired by his father (Big Dave) and grandfather. *Top right:* Don't be surprised to find a line around the block. It's okay—it's just more time to work up an appetite. *Above right:* Come hungry, because the Dave's Way Cheesesteak is no joke.

the grease while enhancing the meat with his own 13-ingredient spice blend. Finally, he achieved that elusive "better than Philly" goal. You don't have to take his word for it, either. In 2018, D won Best Cheesesteak at the World Food Championships.

His cheesesteaks became so popular that neighboring businesses complained about the line outside of the gas station, so, in 2019, D moved operations into a larger space downtown.

The menu favorite has always been the award-winning Dave's Way Cheesesteak Sandwich (your choice of beef, chicken, or salmon, with three cheeses, banana and sweet peppers, mushrooms, and onions).

In addition, Big Dave's offers Philly Fries (french fries loaded up with cheese, onions, and your choice of meats), Cheesesteak Egg Rolls, wings, and—of course—water ice.

To honor the men in his life, D has given back by feeding first responders during the COVID-19 pandemic and by supporting the Black Lives Matter movement.

Downtown:
57 Forsyth St.
404-343-0259

Peachtree Pavilion,
6035 Peachtree Rd., Doraville

thebigdavescheesesteaks.com

CANOE

Riverside dining with a taste from down under

One of the best views in the city is from the patio of Canoe, a riverfront, fine-dining restaurant in Vinings. With the sounds of the cicadas and the river, it's easy to forget you're just 10 minutes from downtown Atlanta. Guests who drive across the city to celebrate special occasions have come to expect exceptional service, regardless of whether they are clad in a tuxedo, a three-piece suit, or T-shirt and shorts.

An Atlanta fine-dining staple for more than 25 years, several of the menu items have become classics. Canoe's House-Smoked Salmon, served on a crispy potato cake with Vermont goat cheese has been on the menu since day one. The Baby Arugula Salad (peppery rocket with spiced nuts, shaved Parmesan, and a poppyseed vinaigrette) and the Marinated Golden and Red Beet Salad (pickled beets with whipped goat cheese, candied walnuts, and basil oil) are so dear to regulars that they've earned a permanent place on the menu.

Other dishes change with the season and with the chef. You'll always find Braised Rabbit Legs with Candied Garlic Sauce, but the accompanying sides change regularly.

The current executive chef, Matthew Basford, has incorporated his Australian roots in the menu. After completing a state-sponsored, four-year apprenticeship in Australia, Matthew moved to New Orleans to cook at Dominique's, in the French Quarter. In 2005, following Hurricane Katrina, he and his wife relocated to Atlanta. Within a week, Matthew was a line cook in the Canoe kitchen. Over the years, he worked his way up through the ranks, and, in 2013, he was named executive chef.

Like the chefs before him, Matthew has added his own stamp to the menu. As any Australian will tell you, a burger isn't complete without a sunny side egg, so he added one to Canoe's Duck 'n' Beef Burger.

Left: With a wall of windows and patio seating facing the Chattahoochee, Canoe has one of the best views in the city. *Center:* Australian-born Chef Basford's Peppercorn Crusted Kangaroo Loin. *Right:* Arrive early to walk along the river and explore the Audubon Society Garden.

But the most notably Australian item on the menu is kangaroo. Unsure how customers would react to eating the marsupial, Matthew initially offered kangaroo as a daily special. It sold out in an hour and a half. Now, kangaroo is a menu mainstay as an appetizer. Mathew says this lean red meat has a taste similar to venison.

With a resident pastry chef, the desserts are not to be missed. The crowd favorite is the Popcorn Ice-Cream Sundae, a parfait of popcorn ice cream, salted caramel sauce, sweetened whipped cream, and Canoe's homemade interpretation of Cracker Jacks.

For one of the best views in the city, take a seat at the outdoor bar, where the whole menu is available. Arrive early to explore the Audubon Society Garden, chicken coop, and beehives.

4199 Paces Ferry Rd. SE
770-432-2663
canoeatl.com

Nestled on the banks of the Chattahoochee River, the brick building was originally a dance hall. During Jim Crow, Robinson's Tropical Gardens was the place to be for white college students, who could dance the night away to live performances by such artists as Little Richard and Otis Redding. And since it was located across the county line in Cobb, students were able to drink at age 18.

DR. BOMBAY'S UNDERWATER TEA PARTY

Supporting girls half a world away

With mismatched furniture, packed bookshelves, and parasols hanging from the ceiling, you may think you've stumbled into an antique shop.

Dr. Bombay's selection of more than 100 teas are presented in vintage teacups and teapots. Baked goods are a mixture of co-owners Katrell Christie's grandmother's Southern recipes (red velvet cake, hummingbird cake, etc.) and Nick Parson's mom's scones.

The star attraction is high tea. When you arrive for the reservation-only experience, you'll find your table set with vintage tablecloths and a tiered cake stand overflowing with an assortment of handmade treats, including sandwiches, quiche, and cakes.

The cafe formerly housed Cold Cream, Katrell's favorite cafe/ice cream shop. When she learned the owner wanted to sell, Katrel, an art restorer, bought the café, renaming it Dr. Bombay's Underwater Tea Party—a reference to playing "tea party" at the bottom of a swimming pool. The original mustache logo was a nod to female artists and authors who worked under a male nom de plume.

Running a coffee shop was harder than she anticipated. Between long hours, slim profits, and staff turnover, she was ready to throw in the towel when a customer invited her on a trip to India.

> Reservations are required for high tea, but individual tea trays (named after Nick's British parents) are available without a reservation. Regulars know about the secret back patio garden, which is just beyond the restrooms.

Left: The used books for sale are just one way Dr. Bombay's supports the Learning Tea.
Center: Tea brings an assortment of baked goods, including cupcakes, cookies, and scones.
Right: Colorful parasols, lanterns, and lamps hang from the ceiling.

Katrell spent her last three weeks in the country volunteering at an orphanage in Darjeeling. There she met three girls who were about to turn 16, when they would age-out of the orphanage. With neither money nor further educational opportunities, the young women faced dim futures. Many girls in such circumstances join the sex trade—or simply disappear. Katrell had no idea how she could help, but she promised she'd return.

Back at the cafe, she put donation jars by the register and hosted a photography exhibit to sell photos from her trip. After six months, she raised enough to go back to India and provide an apartment, food, utilities, and school for the three girls for six months. And she promised to return in another six months to do it again.

Katrell since founded the Learning Tea, a nonprofit that provides necessities for young orphaned women in India. Dr. Bombay supports the nonprofit in a number of ways: collecting and selling used books, donating a portion of the cafe's sales, and hosting a monthly "Taste of India" dinner.

Since 2010, the Learning Tea has helped more than a dozen young women complete college. Four of them have earned master's degrees.

1645 McLendon Ave. NE
404-474-1402
drbombays.com

A social experiment that serves food

It all started with a conversation with his mom. Kevin Gillespie wanted to know why his parents never dined at Woodfire Grill, where he was co-owner and executive chef. Yes, this tasting-menu-only restaurant could easily set a customer back between $200 and $300, but he would happily comp his parents' meals, so the price wasn't the obstacle.

His mom admitted that they were worried they'd embarrass him. They're working-class folks from the country, and they felt out of their element at a high-end, white-tablecloth restaurant. Kevin was crushed.

Inspired by his parents, Kevin envisioned an unpretentious fine-dining experience where everyone would feel comfortable. Which is why you won't find white tablecloths at Gunshow. Instead, the industrial space is outfitted with long communal tables set with bandanas for napkins. The name is a nod to Kevin's father, who worked three jobs, seven days a week, but always made time to attend a monthly flea market/gun show. Kevin told his dad, "I know you'll go to a gun show, so no more excuses."

Gunshow tears down walls, both physically and philosophically. With little separation between the kitchen and the dining room, guests see what goes into making each dish. Instead of a waitstaff that takes orders, each chef presents his or her dishes table-side. Imagine a dim sum restaurant where the chef personally presents each dish to your table. Guests function like judges in a cooking competition, deciding which dishes to try and which to pass on.

This novel concept provides an equally unique experience for cooks. In most restaurants, creating the menu is a privilege reserved for the executive chef, but at Gunshow, the menu is created communally each week. Each cook is assigned a category, say "red meat" or "vegetable." After the Thursday staff lunch, they each present their

Left: Chef Kevin Gillespie doing what he loves best. *Top center:* Each chef offers his or her dish to each table. *Above center:* The chef board shows who is designing which menu item. *Right:* With no room for a bar, drinks are either prepared in the kitchen or on this roaming bar cart.

dish for feedback. From there, they are responsible for ordering ingredients, costing-out the dish, writing the menu description, and, finally, pitching their creation to customers.

You're as likely to see highbrow dishes such as sweetbreads as you are more casual fare such as Frito Pie. Selections remain on the menu for a few weeks at most, depending on ingredient availability. Kevin has one inviolable rule: if you've fallen out of love with the dish you're making, you have to change it. "I don't want anyone cooking something they're not excited about," he says.

But there is one menu staple: Kevin's grandmother's warm banana pudding.

924 Garrett St.
404-380-1886
gunshowatl.com

The menu is designed so that four people can order and share one of everything. If it's just two of you, you'll have to make some hard decisions, but four people should be able to try it all. So bring friends—just not your meat-and-potato friend.

COMMUNITY FARMERS MARKETS

So much more than an outdoor grocery store

With organic produce available 24/7 at grocery stores, at a time when Amazon will deliver groceries right to our door, why do so many Atlantans make a weekly pilgrimage to a neighborhood farmers market? Simple. Because community farmers markets are more than just a place to buy groceries.

They're a place where you can support local farmers and get to know the people who grow your food. You can help the environment by purchasing organic produce with a low carbon footprint while supporting local entrepreneurs.

Farmers markets not only provide a sales channel for local farmers, but they are also an incubator for small businesses. Such vendors as Little Tart Bakeshop, Revolution Doughnuts, Spotted Trotter, and Banjo Coffee got their start at the Grant Park Farmers Market. Not only is vending at the market more affordable than opening a brick-and-mortar store, but the market also draws crowds, giving start-ups invaluable exposure to their brand.

While the stars of the markets are such local farmers as Crack in the Sidewalk and the Middle Georgia Growers Co-Op, man (and woman) does not live by produce alone. At Atlanta's top farmer markets, you will find vendors offering such items as pecan milk, flavored butters, jams, chocolates, local cheeses, fresh pasta, coffee, nut paté, fresh juices, and kombucha.

You'll also find a variety of prepared foods, making the market a convenient place to pick up breakfast, lunch, or a light snack.

Community Farmers Markets (CMF) partners with MARTA (Atlanta's mass transit system) to host weekly markets at stations in

Top left: Even with two brick-and-mortar locations, the Revolution Doughnut tent always has a line of eager customers. *Top right:* The CFM make local foods more accessible by accepting EBT and doubling SNAP dollars. *Above left:* Weekend mornings are meant for strolling around your local farmers market. *Above right:* The chef demos show customers how to cook with seasonal produce.

food deserts (areas with limited access to fresh food). MARTA riders can do their food shopping on their way home. As at other farmers markets, SNAP dollars are doubled at the Fresh MARTA markets.

The biggest appeal of a farmers market is an intangible: farmers markets provide a gathering place where neighbors can come together. The East Atlanta Village Farmers Market, for instance, has a playground and children's activities. You may even find a pop-up library, where the Atlanta-Fulton County Public Library welcomes patrons to obtain a library card or even check out books.

Each season brings its own delights to the city's farmers markets—from peaches in early summer to apples in the fall. More importantly, they provide a Third Place, a place outside of home or work, which nurtures the spirit of community that makes Atlanta unique.

Community Farmers Markets
cfmatl.org

Planes, trains, and ice cream

There's only one spot in the city where you can order ice cream and hot dogs from a little red caboose while watching trains, planes, and automobiles go by.

The Frosty Caboose is a retired Missouri Pacific Rail train caboose, trucked in from Iowa and outfitted as an ice cream stand. It's a fitting tribute to Chamblee, whose motto is "a city on the right track."

The caboose is a must-see for anyone who is into trains. It's located adjacent to the Norfolk Southern Rail tracks and a train repair shop, so passenger and freight trains pass by throughout the day.

There's also a MARTA rail line close by. Overhead, planes intermittently land or take off from DeKalb-Peachtree Airport (PDK), while several car dealerships encourage customers to test-drive new models along this portion of Peachtree. In short, the place is buzzing.

Don't let its size fool you. The Frosty Caboose is a fully functioning ice cream shop, serving up floats, milkshakes, sundaes, and malts. In addition to ice cream, there's sherbet, Italian ice, sorbets, frozen yogurt, and Gourmet Light, (a line of diabetic-friendly ice cream made with Splenda). All the frozen treats are made by local creamery, Greenwood Ice Cream. Nondairy, sugar-free, gluten-free, and egg-free options are available.

In addition to classic flavors, such as chocolate, cookies 'n' cream, vanilla, and rocky road, seasonal flavors appear on the menu. Such yummy flavors as key lime, mango, and lemon custard are offered between March and August, only to make way in September for

Railroad hats and train whistles are for sale at the caboose. Don't leave Rover out! Free dog treats are available–just ask!

Left: A trip to the Frosty Caboose is a must for kids of all ages. *Right:* The Frosty Caboose serves up an assortment of flavors from nearby Greenwood Ice Cream.

such favorites as pumpkin, rum raisin, and apple pie. The sundaes sport railroad-theme names: Sweet Tooth Caboose (1 scoop Vanilla/Chocolate Ice Cream, choice of caramel or chocolate sauce, and M&M's), Polar Express (1 scoop vanilla ice cream, blue topping, and gummy bears), and the Crack in the Track (Rocky Road ice cream, fudge sauce, toasted almonds) each topped with whipped cream and a cherry, of course.

Owner Pam Kachmar also pays homage to her New Jersey roots. On the menu, you'll find New York-style hot dogs with such toppings as onions in red sauce, sauerkraut, spicy mustard, chili, and slaw.

5435 Peachtree Rd.
770-451-4556
frostycaboose.com

Killing it, the Neopolitan way

In much the same way only sparkling wines from the Champagne region of France may be called Champagne, to be considered an authentic Neapolitan pizzeria, an eatery must be certified by the Associazione Verace Pizza Napoletana, which dictates everything from ingredients (preferably from the Campania region) to the cooking (in a woodfire oven kept at at least 806°F).

To comply, many Neapolitan pizzerias in the US import ingredients from Naples. Hugh Connerty, Ammazza's owner, decided it would be truer to the spirit of Neapolitan pizza if he relied on ingredients purchased from local artisans who cure their own meats and make their own cheeses.

"It's meant to be simple and as fresh as possible," says Hugh.

The homemade dough is fermented for three days before being cooked in brick ovens imported from Italy for 90 seconds at 900°F. Instead of importing buffalo mozzarella (made from the milk of water buffalo), Ammazza chefs make their own mozzarella using cow's milk. Whenever possible, Ammazza sources ingredients from local producers, including Spotted Trotter, an Atlanta-based butcher.

While Hugh is committed to the 100-year-old building Ammazza occupies, the location has presented more than its share of challenges. During the pizzeria's first five years, three major construction projects interrupted access. First, Edgewood Avenue was bisected for 13 months while the Edgewood Avenue Bridge was rebuilt. That was followed by construction of the Atlanta Streetcar rail line, and then Google tore up streets to lay fiber cable.

Ammazza offers a vegan menu, featuring their homemade cashew "cheese." Want to spice up your pizza? Add Calabria peppers to your pie.

Left: The Capricciosa—house tomato sauce, marinated artichokes, wild mushrooms, Kalamata olives, Coppa ham, house mozzarella, and fresh basil. *Top center:* The brick ovens, imported from Italy, cook the pizzas at 900°F. *Above center:* The location, at a three-way intersection, has been unlucky. *Right:* The vegan Tartufo—sautéed wild mushrooms, truffle oil, fresh basil, and house-made vegan cashew "cheese."

Hold on! The worst was yet to come.

On the morning of June 10, 2017, a car blasted through the intersection of Randolph Street and Edgewood Avenue, hit a water main, and slammed into the front of the building, causing extensive water damage, which undermined the foundation and rendered the structure uninhabitable. Three weeks later, another car ran into the front of the building!

Instead of moving to another location, Hugh and team decided to rebuild, expanding the kitchen and adding a new counter area—well back from the ill-fated intersection. Twenty-two months later, on March 19, 2019, Ammazza reopened, much to the delight of regulars, old and new.

The word *ammazza*, which comes from the Italian word for a club or bat, means a "killing." It's also Italian slang for "Wow!" Any way you slice it, Ammazza kills it.

591 Edgewood Ave. SE
404-835-2298
ammazza.com

CHOW CLUB ATLANTA

Taste the world, one plate at a time

It's 7 p.m. on Saturday. You arrive at a secret venue, the address having been emailed to you days earlier. You sit at a communal table with strangers. Together, you break bread and learn about a new culture through food. Welcome to Chow Club Atlanta.

Unlike some underground supper clubs that feature a single chef, Chow Club introduces a new chef every month. Cooks share authentic dishes from their native lands. Chefs featured have come from more than 30 countries, including Syria, Antigua, Korea, Afghanistan, Hungary, Morocco, Nigeria, and the Philippines.

When Yohana Solomon cooked a traditional Ethiopian dinner for Amanda Plumb and her friends, the two women realized they were onto something. In 2016, they hosted the first Chow Club dinner in Amanda's house.

The first chef had a restaurant job. What he lacked was a venue where he could show off his skills cooking dishes he grew up with. Thirty people attended the first dinner; several are still regulars.

Ironically, as Washington made it increasingly difficult for immigrants, Chow Club ticket sales skyrocketed. Patrons were eager to support immigrant chefs and learn about their cultures.

"When someone shares food that they've made from scratch, it's hard to see them as 'illegal.' Food helps us recognize our shared humanity," says Yohana.

Chow Club provides a low-risk venue for aspiring chefs to build their own brand. Basically, they buy the ingredients and agree to share their story with guests. Yohana and Amanda take care of marketing, the venue, and everything else.

"As a new immigrant chef, I needed support and someone familiar with the local pop-up scene. Chow Club provided all that," says Amal, a home-cook from Afghanistan.

Left: Kettley Jeantty prepares patties for her Haitian brunch. Photo by Patrick Di Rito. *Top center:* Guests sit at shared tables where they quickly make new friends. Photo by Stephen Nowland. *Above center:* Chow Club cofounders Amanda Plumb and Yohana Solomon with a Chow Club passport. Photo by Catie Leary. *Right:* Fu-Mao Sun shows off one of the dishes in his Taiwanese menu. Photo by Haley Zapal.

Each month, members receive an email with the menu for the upcoming dinner and a link to buy tickets. Members receive a passport, and, at each dinner, they collect a stamp representing the cuisine of the evening. Ambassadors, guests with five or more stamps, may purchase tickets before they go on sale to the public.

First-time guests come because of the food. They return because of the fellowship, the chance to learn about a different culture—and the food.

"It's always a lively, fun evening," says regular Sarah Logan Gregory. "It's become a highlight of my eating adventures. While restaurants do offer various ethnic cuisines, none offer the personal experience of a Chow Club dinner."

The location is secret!
Sign up online for more information.
chowclubatlanta.com

Dinners can sell out quickly, so purchase tickets as soon as possible. Chefs always offer vegan and gluten-free alternatives and try to accommodate all dietary restrictions.

A simple name for a simple place

Bob Hatcher's restaurant experience was limited to dishwashing when he followed longtime friend Charlie Kerns to Atlanta in 1981. After his job as plant manager of Georgia's only record-pressing plant fell victim to the rise of CDs, Bob signed on as a manager at Tortillas, Charlie's mission-style burrito joint and darling of Atlanta's indie scene.

The old friends wanted to open a second eatery, but the problem was real estate. "If we liked it, we couldn't afford it. And if we could afford it, we didn't like it," remembers Bob.

The only affordable location they could find, a former nightclub called Frank's Place, was less than a half-mile from Tortillas—too close for a second burrito joint. Charlie's solution? Create a small food court with separate counters offering a variety of cuisines. He envisioned a menu that would appeal to a broad range of tastes, from fresh vegetables for the vegetarians, baked chicken (jerk, lemon pepper, or BBQ) for folks who wanted to eat healthy, and home-cooked pasta sauces (which have since been taken off the menu).

The $10,000 each put in soon ran out, so Bob and Charlie were forced to open Eats even before they finished building out the space. In fact, they never built the sandwich counter that was originally part of the Eats concept.

Over the years, Bob has displayed a number of photographs of Atlanta residents and landmarks. One of his prized possessions is an autographed copy of *The Adventures of Blondie Strange*, a comic book about the Clairmont Lounge's most famous performer. When an employee moved from Washington State to Atlanta, she donated an old vanity license plate (007 Diva) for wall art. Customers soon followed suit.

Top left: Jerk chicken, corn, sweet potato, collards, and cornbread. *Above left:* The Chicken Lasagna comes with garlic bread and a salad. *Top right:* Despite all the gentrification, Eats has been a fixture on Ponce de Leon since 1993. *Above right:* Known for their large portions and reasonable prices, Eats is a lunchtime favorite.

Early on, Eats served cafeteria style. Customers would order at a counter and bring their food to the register to check out before sitting down to eat. Because some people figured out how to game the system, customers now pay when they order.

Eats is well known for its reasonable prices. Bob credits Charlie with this. "Charlie didn't want to gouge people. It's simple food, and he wanted to sell it for as little as possible and still make a decent profit," Bob says. Perhaps that's why Eats draws a diverse crowd that Bob describes as "a slice of society." Customers include construction workers, business people, and public officials as well as people who are homeless and an occasional celebrity.

While Ponce is rapidly changing, Eats remains a neighborhood staple. And since Bob bought the building in the late '90s, it likely will remain a local institution for the foreseeable future.

Bob and Charlie no longer work together, but Bob credits Charlie with the concept. And he cherishes the relationships he's formed with staff, customers, and neighbors.

600 Ponce de Leon Ave.
404-888-9149
eatsonponce.net

MORELLI'S ICE CREAM

Sweet dreams are made of these

Ever since his first job at an ice cream parlor in Tampa, Florida, Donald Sargent dreamed of opening his own ice cream store. He studied hotel and restaurant management in college and continued working in the hospitality industry after graduation. But he found himself working 70 hours a week and making a fraction of what his friends in sales were making. So Donald quit "the industry" and moved on to more profitable pharmaceutical sales and real estate investing.

While on vacation in Brazil in 2004, Donald met Clarissa Morelli, a local college student vacationing with friends. He was so smitten that he decided to move to Brazil to be near her. But when housing prices dropped in late 2006, Donald moved to Atlanta to salvage a few of his rental properties. Despite his best efforts, the bank foreclosed. Donald filed for bankruptcy and returned to pharmaceutical sales. A year later, Clarissa moved to the US to be with him.

In 2008, Donald saw an opportunity to return to his childhood dream when a Bruster's Ice Cream on Moreland went out of business. The couple took over the lease and purchased the existing equipment. Clarissa, eight months pregnant at the time, ran the shop during the day, while Donald worked his sales job. In the evenings, Donald took over the store.

"It was so much fun, I decided to never go back to pharmaceutical sales," he remembers.

The ice cream parlor was Donald's dream, but Clarissa had a huge influence from the beginning. The store bears her last name because the couple agreed "Morelli's" sounded better than "Sargent's." Many of the flavors, such as Sweet Corn and Guava Cream Cheese, are inspired by her Brazilian roots.

Left: In addition to traditional flavors, you'll find more original creations such as Flan Caramello and Rosemary Olive Oil. *Top right:* Husband and wife team Donald Sargent and Clarissa Morelli have combined Donald's dream to own an ice cream parlor with flavors inspired by Clarissa's home in Brazil. *Above right:* Coconut Jalapeño ice cream blends sweet and spicy for an unforgettable taste. Photos by Haley Zapal.

Although Morelli's had been open for only a year at the time, *Bon Appetit* magazine named it 4th-Best Ice Cream Shop in America!

Donald says their secret is "we're always honest to the ice cream," meaning they use the highest-quality ingredients. Morelli's uses a cream with a high percentage of fat and a gelato machine that does not whip a lot of air into the ice cream. The result is a rich, dense ice cream. They grate fresh ginger for the Ginger Lavender, brew tea for Earl Grey, cook-down fresh bananas for the Banana Cream Pie, and—of course—their Krispie Kreamier is made with chunks of real Krispy Kreme doughnuts.

749 Moreland Ave. SE
404-622-0210
morellisicecream.com

Check the website and Facebook for the current list of flavors. While only 15 flavors are displayed, if it's not too busy, ask what flavors they have in the back freezer. Donald bakes his mom's 7-Up Pound Cake each week. Stop by on Tuesday evening for the freshest slice.

RESTAURANTS BY NEIGHBORHOOD

RESTAURANTS A-Z

57th Fighter Group Restaurant, 138
3829 Clairmont Rd.

Ammazza, 184
591 Edgewood Ave. SE

Ann's Snack Bar, 40
1615 Memorial Dr. SE

Atlanta Chinatown Mall, 70
5383 New Peachtree Rd.

Bacchanalia & Star Provisions, 4
1460 Ellsworth Industrial Blvd., Suite A

Batavia, 132
3640 Shallowford Rd.

Bell Street Burritos, 2
1816 Peachtree St.
4053 Lawrenceville Hwy.
112 Krog St. NE

Big Dave's Cheesesteak, 172
57 Forsyth St.
6035 Peachtree Rd.

Botiwalla, 118
675 Ponce De Leon Ave. NE

BrewAble Café, 74
175 Roswell St.

Buford Highway, 122
Various locations

The Busy Bee Cafe, 14
810 Martin Luther King Jr. Dr. SW

Café Intermezzo, 148
1065 Peachtree St., Suite 2
4505 Ashford-Dunwoody Rd.
100 Avalon Blvd.

Cafe Sunflower, 46
2140 Peachtree Rd. NW

Canoe, 174
4199 Paces Ferry Rd. SE

Central Food Hall at Ponce City Market, 160
675 Ponce de Leon Ave. N

Chai Pani, 118
406 W Ponce de Leon Ave.

Chow Club Atlanta, 186
The location is secret!

The Colonnade, 158
1879 Cheshire Bridge Rd. NE

Community Farmers Markets, 180
Various locations

Crawfish Shack, 28
4337 Buford Hwy. NE

Delia's Chicken Sausage Stand, 164
489 Moreland Ave. SE
881 Marietta St. NW

Dr. Bombay's Underwater Tea Party, 176
1645 McLendon Ave. NE

Dutch Monkey Doughnuts, 12
3075 Ronald Reagan Blvd.

Eats, 188
600 Ponce de Leon Ave.

El Burro Pollo, 130
756 W. Peachtree St. NW

El Rey Del Taco, 66
5288 Buford Hwy.

El Super Pan, 130
Ponce City Market,
675 Ponce de Leon Ave.
455 Legends Place SE.

Elmyr, 76
1091 Euclid Ave. NE

Emerald City Bagels, 68
1257-A Glenwood Ave. SE

Flying Biscuit, 116
1655 McLendon Ave.
Various locations

Frosty Caboose, 182
5435 Peachtree Rd.

Giving Kitchen, 110
givingkitchen.org

Gunshow, 178
924 Garrett St.

Gu's Dumplings, 166
99 Krog St. NE
6330 Halcyon Way

Gu's Kitchen, 166
4897 Buford Hwy.

Havana Sandwich Shop, 156
2905 Buford Hwy. NE

Heirloom Market BBQ, 50
2243 Akers Mill Rd.

Holeman & Finch Public House, 42
1197 Peachtree St. NE, Suite 160

il Localino, 16
467 North Highland Ave. NE

Kimball House, 78
303 E. Howard Ave.

Krog Street Market, 52
99 Krog St. NE

Lazy Betty, 108
1530 DeKalb Ave. NE

Little Bear, 126
71 Georgia Ave. SE, Suite A

Little's Food Store, 162
198 Carroll St.

Mamak, 150
2390 Chamblee Tucker Rd.

Manuel's Tavern, 56
602 North Highland Ave.

Marcel, 38
1170 Howell Mill Rd.

Mary Mac's Tea Room, 64
224 Ponce De Leon
Ave. NE

Masterpiece, 18
3940 Buford Hwy.
11625 Medlock Bridge Rd.

Mi Barrio, 10
571 Memorial Dr. SE

Miller Union, 32
999 Brady Ave. NW

Morelli's Ice Cream, 190
749 Moreland Ave. SE

Nick's Food To Go, 48
240 Martin Luther King Jr
Dr. SE

Octopus Bar, 38
560 Gresham Ave. SE

**Paolo's Gelato
Italiano, 136**
1025 Virginia Ave.

Patel Plaza, 102
1709 Church St.

Plaza Fiesta, 20
4166 Buford Hwy. NE

**R. Thomas Deluxe
Grill, 144**
1812 Peachtree St. NW

Refuge Coffee Co., 54
4170 E. Ponce de
Leon Ave.
145 Auburn Ave. NE

Ria's Bluebird, 44
421 Memorial Dr. SE

**Shakespheare's Tavern
Playhouse, 60**
499 Peachtree St NE

The Silver Skillet, 170
200 14th St. NW

Snackboxe Bistro, 142
6035 Peachtree Rd.,
Ste C114

**Sevananda Natural
Foods Market, 34**
467 Moreland Ave. NE

Soul Veg, 72
879 Ralph David
Abernathy Blvd. SW
652 N. Highland Ave.

Spring, 8
90 Marietta Station
Walk NE

**Starlight Drive-In and
Flea Market, 146**
2000 Moreland Ave.

Sublime Doughnuts, 62
535 10th St. NW
2566 Briarcliff Rd. NE

Sushi Hayakawa, 58
5979 Buford Hwy. NE

**Sweet Auburn
Barbecue, 106**
656 North Highland Ave.
Sweet Auburn Curb Market,
209 Edgewood Ave.

**Sweet Auburn Curb
Market, 106**
209 Edgewood Ave. SE

**Sweet Hut & Food
Terminal, 80**
Various locations

Talat Market, 128
112 Ormond St. S

**The Tamarind
Group, 36**
Various locations

Taqueria del Sol, 134
Various locations

Ticonderoga Club, 152
99 Krog St. NE

**Twisted Soul Cookhouse
& Pours, 114**
1133 Huff Rd. NW #D

The Varsity, 24
Various locations

**Virgil's Gullah Kitchen
& Bar, 140**
3721 Main St.

The Vortex, 120
878 Peachtree St. NE
438 Moreland Ave.

We Suki Suki, 154
477 Flat Shoals Rd.

The White Bull, 82
123 E. Court Square

**W. H. Stiles Fish Camp
in Ponce City Market, 4**
675 Ponce de Leon Ave.

Watchman's, 78
99 Krog St. NE

**Xocolatl Small Batch
Chocolate, 168**
99 Krog St. NE

**Your DeKalb Farmers
Market, 112**
3000 E. Ponce de Leon
Ave.